# modern
# BABY

## EASY, FRESH, AND FUN
## QUILT DESIGNS

Martingale
*Create with Confidence*

Modern Baby: Easy, Fresh, and Fun Quilt Designs
© 2013 by Martingale®

Martingale
19021 120th Ave. NE, Ste. 102
Bothell, WA 98011-9511 USA
ShopMartingale.com

Printed in China
18 17 16 15 14 13          8 7 6 5 4 3 2 1

Library of Congress Cataloging-in-Publication Data is available upon request.

ISBN: 978-1-60468-278-6

## MISSION STATEMENT
**Dedicated to providing quality products and service to inspire creativity.**

## CREDITS
President & CEO: Tom Wierzbicki

Editor in Chief: Mary V. Green

Design Director: Paula Schlosser

Managing Editor: Karen Costello Soltys

Acquisitions Editor: Karen M. Burns

Technical Editor: Rebecca Kemp Brent

Copy Editor: Melissa Bryan

Production Manager: Regina Girard

Illustrator: Christine Erikson

Cover & Text Designer: Adrienne Smitke

Photographer: Brent Kane

# Contents

# Welcome Little Ones!

Baby quilts come in all shapes, sizes, textures, and colors nowadays. Think a quilt for a baby girl needs to be pink? Think again! Or that a baby boy needs to have trucks or dinosaurs on his quilt? Uh-uh. Today's quilts, whether categorized as traditional, contemporary, modern—or anywhere in between—are just as varied (and just as delightful) as the lucky babies who will receive them.

When I had children, one of my family members gave each of my girls a baby quilt. Those quilts went everywhere with us—comforting the girls at night, lying with them on the floor for tummy time, cushioning their falls when they were learning to crawl and walk, and wrapping them with warmth as they watched Saturday morning cartoons on the couch. Their quilts were well-loved and became softer with each wash after ice cream, cereal, and other spills. Because those quilts provided such comfort, happiness, and joy to my girls, I decided it would be nice to assist others in discovering the delight of making a unique baby quilt for your own baby or as a gift for a special new arrival.

It has been such a pleasure to work with so many talented quilt designers to fill the pages of *Modern Baby*. Many of these women are moms themselves with young children and babies. So who would know better about making a huggable baby quilt? From asymmetrical and improvisational piecing to foundation piecing and appliqué, I'm sure you'll find enough fabulous project options in this book to fulfill all of your baby shower needs for several years to come.

In fact, we had so many wonderful projects to choose from, that we decided to omit all of the basic quiltmaking information that we usually include in our books. You can find all the help you need at ShopMartingale.com/HowtoQuilt. The information is free and easy to download. And by putting it online for you, it gave us room to include at least one more project.

Now, what are you waiting for? Let's get sewing. I can't think of a better way to welcome a special little child into the world than with his or her special handmade quilt. Can you?

~ Karen M. Burns
Acquisitions Editor, Martingale

# Busy Blocks

Vivid solids are a great choice for a baby quilt. The bold colors grow with the child and keep this quilt in use for years! Use the solid fabrics to showcase unique machine quilting in each block.

~ Shea

> **» Fabric Facts**
>
> All fabrics in the sample quilt are Robert Kaufman Kona Cotton Solids: Chartreuse, Fern, Peacock, and Nightfall for blocks; Lime, Cactus, Robin Egg, and Pacific for block centers; and Nightfall again for binding and backing.

## MATERIALS

*Yardage is based on 42"-wide fabric and includes fabric for a pieced backing as instructed below.*

1 yard of green solid for blocks and backing (fabric A)

1 yard of navy solid for blocks and binding (fabric C)

¾ yard of bright-green solid for blocks (fabric D)

⅝ yard of bright-blue solid for blocks (fabric B)

¼ yard *each* of 4 assorted solids for block centers (Choose fabrics in the same color families but lighter values than the block fabrics; these are fabrics 1–4.)

½ yard of white solid for blocks

2 yards of fabric for backing

52" x 52" piece of batting

## CUTTING

*A ¼" seam allowance is included in all measurements.*

### From *each* of fabrics A–C, cut:

3 strips, 4" x 42"; crosscut into 20 squares, 4" x 4" (60 total)

2 strips, 4½" x 42"; crosscut into 10 squares, 4½" x 4½" (30 total; 1 B square will be extra)

5 strips, 2¼" x 42", *from fabric C only*

### From fabric D, cut:

4 strips, 4" x 42"; crosscut into 28 squares, 4" x 4" (Reserve 4 for pieced backing.)

2 strips, 4½" x 42"; crosscut into 13 squares, 4½" x 4½"

### From *each* of fabrics 1–3, cut:

1 strip, 4" x 42"; crosscut into 6 squares, 4" x 4" (18 total)

### From fabric 4, cut:

1 strip, 4" x 42"; crosscut into 8 squares, 4" x 4" (Reserve 1 for pieced backing.)

### From the white fabric, cut:

3 strips, 4" x 42"; crosscut into 24 squares, 4" x 4"

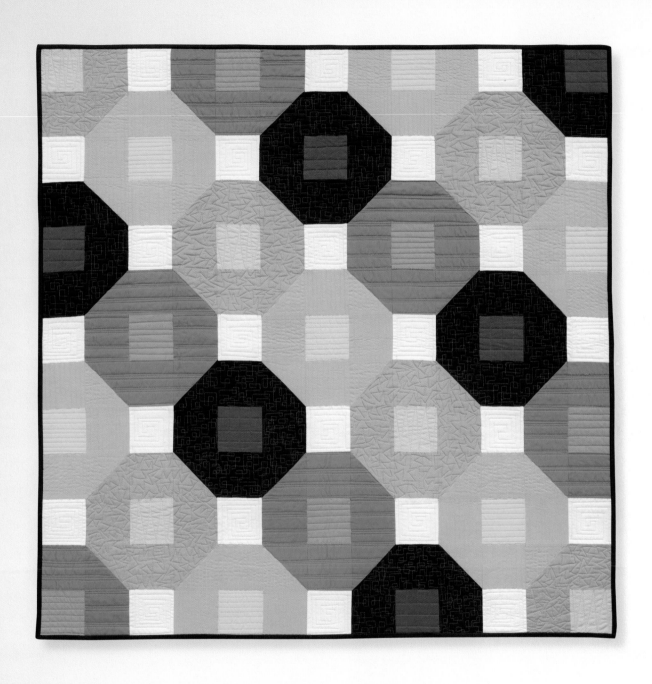

Designed and made by Shea Henderson

## MAKING THE BLOCKS

**1.** Stack the 4½" squares in pairs, right sides together, as listed below:

A and B: 2 pairs

A and C: 4 pairs

A and D: 4 pairs

B and C: 2 pairs

B and D: 5 pairs

C and D: 4 pairs.

**2.** Mark a diagonal line from corner to corner on the wrong side of the lighter fabric in each pair. Stitch each pair of squares together, sewing ¼" from the diagonal line on each side.

Mark.          Stitch.

### » Time for a Chain

To save time, chain piece all the pairs by sewing along one side of the line, and then turn the chain of pieces around and sew in the opposite direction along the other side of the marked lines. Before proceeding to the next step, snip the threads to separate the chain-pieced squares.

**3.** Press the squares flat as sewn, and then cut each pair of squares in half on the marked line. Trim the dog-ears (corners) and press the units open, pressing the seam allowances toward the darker fabric. Trim each unit to 4" x 4". You will have 42 half-square-triangle units. Reserve two A/D and two C/D units for the pieced backing. One A/D and one C/D unit will be left over.

Cut.          Press open.

## ASSEMBLING THE QUILT TOP

**1.** Arrange the plain 4" squares and the half-square-triangle units in 13 rows of 13 units each, referring to the quilt assembly diagram. Correct placement and orientation of each unit is essential to form the O shapes in the quilt layout.

**2.** Sew the units together into rows, pressing the seam allowances open to reduce bulk later. (Or you can press to one side, if you prefer.)

### » Pressing Open

Shea favors pressing seam allowances open in this quilt design to reduce bulk in the quilt top. While joining blocks and rows, she pins exactly at the seam intersections to match points perfectly.

**3.** Sew the rows together, pinning at all seams. Press the seam allowances open.

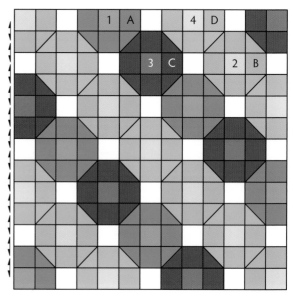

Quilt assembly

## ASSEMBLING THE BACKING

To coordinate with the quilt front, Shea made an additional pieced block, and set it into a pieced quilt backing. You can follow her lead for a fun quilt backing, or use a plain backing if you're in a hurry!

### ADDITIONAL CUTTING

**From the backing fabric, cut:**
1 rectangle, 32" x 53"
1 rectangle, 10" x 53"
1 rectangle, 9" x 11"

**From the remainder of fabric A, cut:**
1 strip, 11" x 34"

> ## » Width Wise

Cut the two 53" lengths of backing fabric by splitting the fabric lengthwise into approximately 10" and 32" sections. If the fabric is a bit less than 42" wide, the backing will be slightly smaller than the batting, but it will still be large enough to finish the quilt. It's okay to include the selvages in these width measurements, as they will be trimmed away before the quilt binding is added.

## PIECING THE BACK

**1.** Using the reserved half-square-triangle units, fabric D squares, and fabric 4 square, assemble one block.

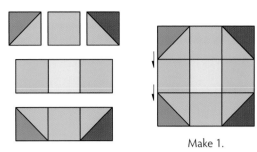

Make 1.

**2.** Sew the fabric A strip to the side of the block with A/D units, and add the 9" x 11" rectangle of fabric C to the opposite side of the block. Pin and then sew the long fabric C pieces to the top and bottom of the pieced strip as shown. Press the seam allowances away from the pieced block.

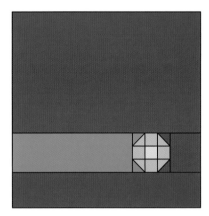

Pieced quilt back

## FINISHING THE QUILT

For more information on finishing techniques, go to ShopMartingale.com/HowtoQuilt for free illustrated instructions.

**1.** Prepare the backing.

**2.** Layer the quilt top, batting, and backing, and baste the layers together. Be sure the quilt top is centered and aligned with the pieced quilt backing. Quilt as desired.

**3.** Trim the backing and batting to match the quilt top.

**4.** Use the 2¼"-wide strips of fabric C to bind the edges of the quilt. Add a label (if desired).

# Floating Pyramid

This quilt was born from the idea of making bright fabric-scrap triangles that seem to hover above a background of neutrals. I chose different values of each main color to create scrappy 60° triangles, and then pieced them into a large pyramid. This was set against a background pieced from solid 60° triangles of four different neutral fabrics. The end result is a beautiful, colorful pyramid that appears to be floating!

~Audrie

> **» Fabric Facts**
>
> Neutral fabrics in the sample quilt are Robert Kaufman Kona Cotton Solids (White, Natural, and Snow) and Moda Bella Solid (Feather).

## MATERIALS

*Yardage is based on 42"-wide fabric.*

⅛ yard or large scraps *each* of 7 assorted colors, including 4 to 7 different fabrics per color, for triangles

¾ yard *each* of 4 different neutral solids for background

½ yard of neutral fabric for binding

3⅛ yards of fabric for backing

55" x 66" piece of batting

Template plastic

60° triangle ruler, 6" size (optional)

## CUTTING

*A ¼" seam allowance is included in all measurements. Patterns are on pages 14–15.*

> **» Ruler Rules**
>
> If you're using the optional 60° triangle ruler, follow the manufacturer's instructions to substitute the ruler for the pattern pieces.

**From the assortment of fabrics in 7 colors, cut:**
Randomly sized squares and rectangles ranging from 1½" to 3" in each dimension

**From *each* of the neutral solids, cut:**
4 strips, 6½" x 42"; crosscut into 27 triangles using pattern A (108 total; 3 triangles will be left over) and 3 triangles *each* using patterns B and C (12 total *of each*; 2 B triangles and 2 C triangles will be left over)

**From the neutral fabric for binding, cut:**
6 strips, 2¼" x 42"

Designed and pieced by Audrie Bidwell; quilted by Laura McCarrick

## MAKING THE BLOCKS

**1.** Sew assorted fabric pieces of one color into a row at least 8" long. Press the seam allowances to one side as you go to ensure the row lies flat. Trim the top and bottom edges of the row to neaten; the cuts do not have to be parallel.

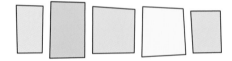

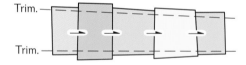

**2.** Create a slightly shorter row of the same color and sew it to the top of the first row, matching the row centers. Check the assembly against the triangle A pattern to be sure the piecing is larger than the pattern. Continue adding rows to create a pieced triangle at least 8" wide at the base and 7½" high.

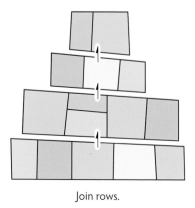

Join rows.

**3.** Trace the patterns on pages 14–15 onto template plastic and cut out. Use the triangle A template to cut one triangle from the pieced unit. Repeat the process to make four triangles each from four colors and three triangles each from three colors, for a total of 25 scrappy triangles.

## ASSEMBLING THE QUILT TOP

**1.** Referring to the quilt assembly diagram, right, arrange the scrappy triangles on your design wall. Position the colors as shown or as desired.
**2.** Position the neutral triangles around the floating pyramid, arranging the individual fabrics to achieve a nice mix. Add the B and C triangles to the row ends.
**3.** Sew the triangles together into rows.

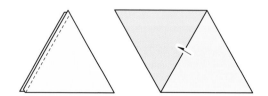

**4.** Sew the rows together, matching the points and intersecting seams. Trim and square the quilt top before quilting.

## FINISHING THE QUILT

For more information on finishing techniques, go to ShopMartingale.com/HowtoQuilt for free illustrated instructions.

**1.** Prepare the backing.

**2.** Layer the quilt top, batting, and backing, and baste the layers together. Quilt as desired.

**3.** Trim the backing and batting to match the quilt top.

**4.** Use the neutral 2¼"-wide strips to bind the edges of the quilt. Add a label (if desired).

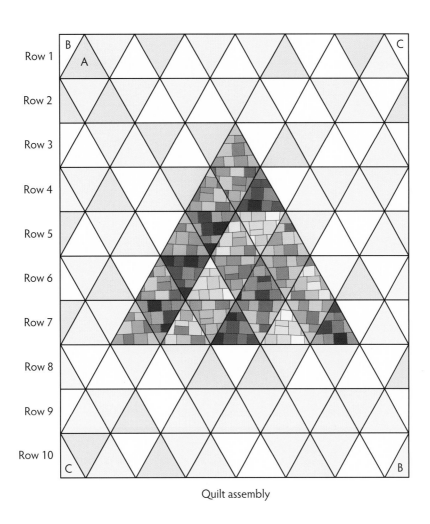

Quilt assembly

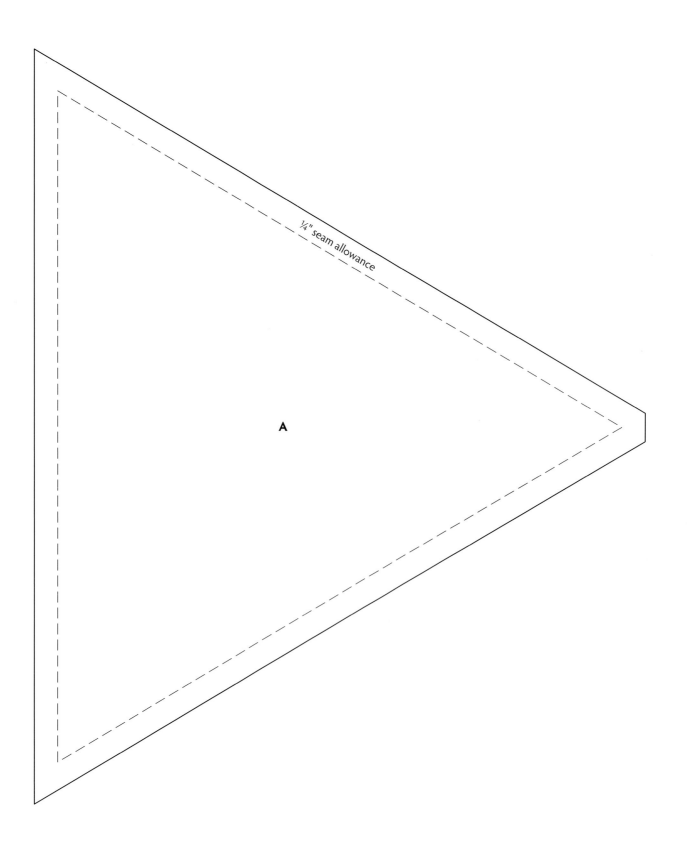

¼" seam allowance

A

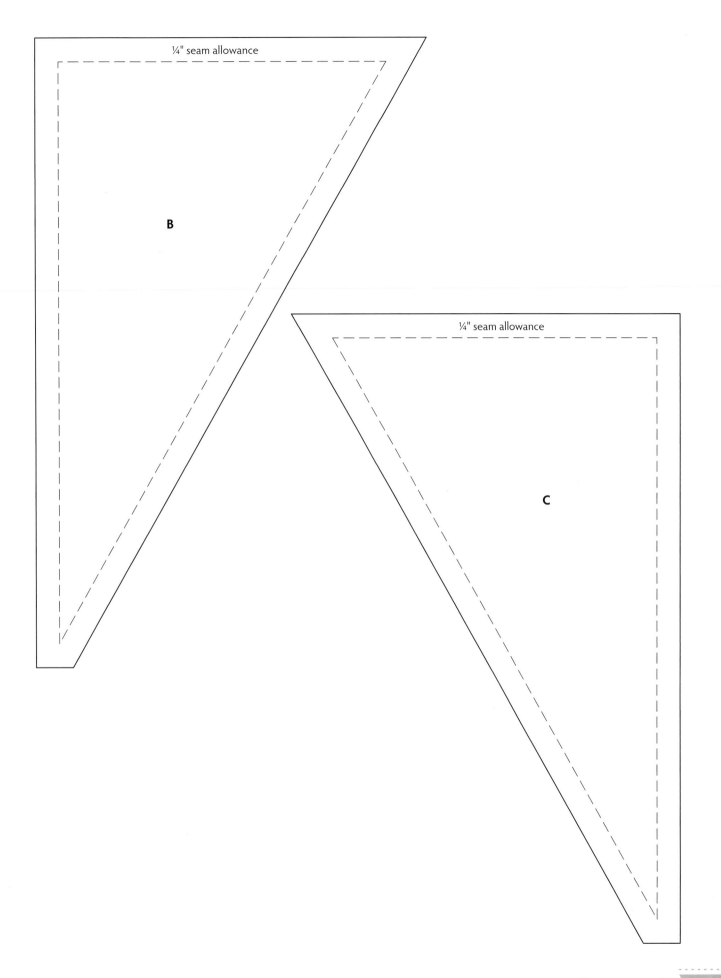

¼" seam allowance

B

¼" seam allowance

C

# Tiny Textured Trees

This quilt is all about trees, texture, and a super-soft, but vibrant, color palette. I used a variety of fabrics for the trees—sateen, linen, corduroy, silk, and cotton—to create a tactile treat for tiny tots to enjoy.

~Carolyn

## » Fabric Facts

- Textured fabrics in the sample quilt are all from Robert Kaufman.

- Prewash and dry all fabrics, especially when using a variety of fibers or fabric types.

- Follow the cutting diagram if using corduroy so the wales will run in the correct direction.

- If desired, use leftover block fabrics for a scrappy binding. Cut 2¼"-wide strips and sew them together end to end; press the seam allowances open.

## MATERIALS

*Yardage is based on 42"-wide fabric. Corduroy option is based on 57"-wide fabric.*

1 yard of ivory solid for sashing*

⅞ yard of lime-green solid for border and binding

¼ yard OR 1 fat quarter *each* of 5 assorted green prints for block backgrounds

¼ yard OR 1 fat quarter *each* of 5 assorted ivory fabrics for blocks*

1½ yards of fabric for backing

46" x 49" piece of batting

*For corduroy option, purchase 1⅛ yards of ivory corduroy for blocks and sashing plus 4 assorted ivory fat quarters or ¼-yard cuts.*

## CUTTING

*A ¼" seam allowance is included in all measurements.*

### From the ivory solid, cut:*
1 strip, 7" x 35" (A)
1 strip, 2½" x 35" (B)
3 strips, 2" x 31½" (C)
2 strips, 2" x 25" (D)
16 rectangles, 2" x 5½" (E)

*Continued on page 18*

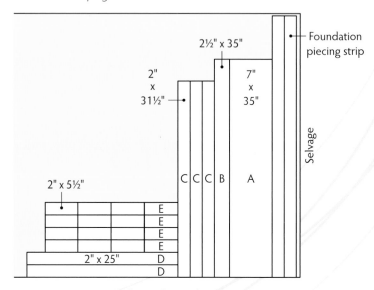

Cutting layout for corduroy

Designed and made by Carolyn Friedlander

From the lime-green solid, cut:
2 strips, 3" x 33½"
1 strip, 3" x 39½"
1 strip, 7½" x 39½"
5 strips, 2¼" x 42"

From the assorted green prints, cut:
3½" x 42" strips as needed for foundation piecing

From the assorted ivory fabrics, cut:
2" x 42" strips as needed for foundation piecing

## MAKING THE BLOCKS

**1.** Make 20 copies of each foundation pattern on page 19. Martingale's Papers for Foundation Piecing, newsprint, or lightweight office paper work well.

### » Firm Foundations

Shorten your sewing machine's stitch length to 1.5 mm, or 18 stitches per inch. This creates a tight seam and perforates the foundation paper nicely for easy removal. For more information on paper foundation piecing, go to ShopMartingale.com/HowtoQuilt for free illustrated instructions.

**2.** Following basic methods for paper foundation piecing, make block sections A and B using assorted green-print strips for the background (areas marked 1, 3, and 5) and assorted ivory strips for the tree (areas marked 2, 4, and 6). Trim each section ¼" outside the printed outer seam line.

**3.** Sew an A section to each B section, matching the corners and sewing along the foundation seam line.

Match corners.

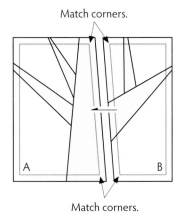

Match corners.

**4.** Remove the foundation paper within the seam allowances and press them toward section A. Make 20 blocks.

### » Foundation-Piecing Basics

For more information on foundation piecing, go to ShopMartingale.com/HowtoQuilt, where you can download free illustrated instructions.

## ASSEMBLING THE QUILT TOP

Refer to the quilt assembly diagram below as needed. Remove the paper from the seam allowances after sewing each seam.

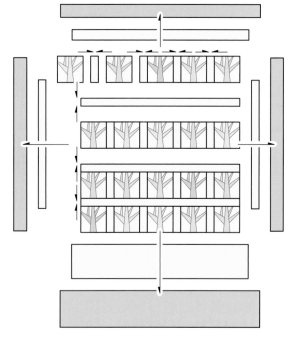

Quilt assembly

### » Sewing with Corduroy

Pin the borders and corduroy sashing pieces in place before sewing. For even feeding through the machine, sew the pieces together with the corduroy on the bottom and the foundation paper on the top.

**1.** Arrange the blocks in four rows of five blocks each, inserting the sashing E rectangles between the blocks. Sew the pieces together into rows, and press the seam allowances toward the sashing.

**2.** Sew the rows together, alternating them with the sashing C strips, and then add sashing D strips to both sides. Press the seam allowances toward the sashing strips.

**3.** Sew sashing-strip B to the top edge and sashing-strip A to the bottom. Press the seam allowances toward the sashing.

**4.** Sew the lime-green 3" x 33½" border strips to the sides of the quilt top. Add the 3" x 39½" border strip to the top edge and the 7½" x 39½" border strip to the bottom edge. Press the seam allowances toward the border strips.

**5.** Carefully remove the remaining foundation paper from the blocks.

## FINISHING THE QUILT

For more information on finishing techniques, go to ShopMartingale.com/HowtoQuilt for free illustrated instructions.

**1.** Prepare the backing.

**2.** Layer the quilt top, batting, and backing, and baste the layers together. Quilt as desired.

**3.** Trim the backing and batting to match the quilt top.

**4.** Use the lime-green 2¼"-wide strips to bind the edges of the quilt. Add a label (if desired).

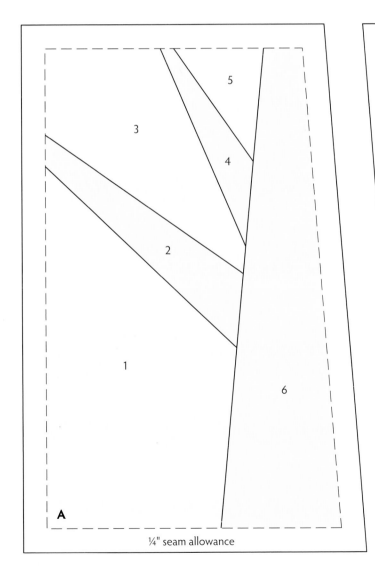

A

¼" seam allowance

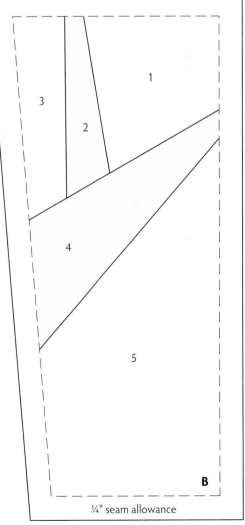

B

¼" seam allowance

# Daddy's Little Girl

**FINISHED QUILT: 40" x 40"   FINISHED BLOCK: 4" x 4"**

This vivacious quilt puts a modern spin on a traditional zigzag pattern. While the focus is on the vertical zigzags, horizontal bands of varied background fabrics create a fun, unique juxtaposition. Fading the background from black to white—with dark gray in the middle—increases this effect and makes the pink zigzags pop. The appliquéd letters provide a soft counterpoint to the angles, spelling out a sentiment that leaves no doubt about the recipient of this sweet stunner.

~ Melissa

## » Fabric Facts

Fabrics are from Riley Blake Designs: black-and-white prints are from the Tuxedo Collection by Doodlebug Design and the pink print is from Cotton Candy Basic Shades. Together they create the perfect mix.

## MATERIALS

*Yardage is based on 42"-wide fabric.*

1⅛ yard of pink print for blocks, appliqués, and binding

⅓ yard of darkest black print for blocks and setting triangles

¼ yard *each* of 5 prints ranging from black, to gray, to white for blocks and setting triangles

¼ yard of lightest white print for blocks and setting triangles

1¼ yards of fabric for backing

46" x 46" piece of batting

Paper-backed fusible web

Coordinating thread for appliqué

## CUTTING

*A ¼" seam allowance is included in all measurements unless otherwise specified.*

### From the pink print, cut:
78 rectangles, 2½" x 4½"
5 strips, 2¼" x 42"

### From the darkest black print, cut:
2 squares, 7½" x 7½"; cut into quarters diagonally to yield 8 side triangles
1 square, 4¼" x 4¼"; cut in half diagonally to yield 2 corner triangles
1 square, 4½" x 4½"
12 rectangles, 2½" x 4½"

### From *each* of the assorted prints, cut:
1 square, 7½" x 7½"; cut into quarters diagonally to yield 4 side triangles (20 total; 2 triangles of each print will be left over)
1 square, 4½" x 4½" (5 total)
12 rectangles, 2½" x 4½" (60 total)

### From the lightest white print, cut:
2 squares, 7½" x 7½"; cut into quarters diagonally to yield 8 side triangles (2 will be left over)
1 square, 4¼" x 4¼"; cut in half diagonally to yield 2 corner triangles
1 square, 4½" x 4½"
6 rectangles, 2½" x 4½"

Designed and made by Melissa Corry

## MAKING THE BLOCKS

Sew a pink-print rectangle to each black, gray, and white rectangle. Press the seam allowances away from the pink rectangles. Make 78 total.

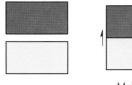

Make 78.

## ASSEMBLING THE QUILT TOP

**1.** Arrange the pieced blocks as shown, adding the 4½" squares and setting triangles. Assemble the quilt top in 13 diagonal rows, carefully maintaining block placement and orientation. Press the seam allowances toward unbroken patches to reduce bulk.

> **» Triangle Tips**
>
> The setting triangles have been cut oversized to allow for trimming after assembly. Align the side triangles along one edge of each row, allowing overhang along the opposite edge of the row. Center each corner triangle with equal overhang on each side of the block.

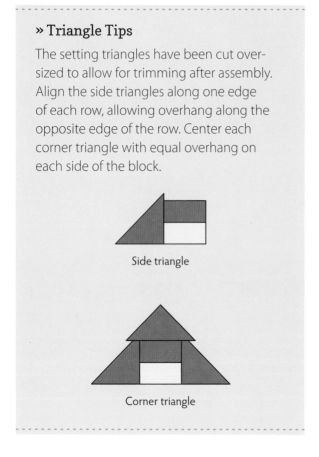

Side triangle

Corner triangle

**2.** Sew the rows together and press all the seam allowances in one direction. Sew the setting triangles to the corners and press the seam allowances toward the triangles.

Quilt assembly

**3.** Using a rotary cutter and ruler, trim excess fabric from the setting triangles, leaving ¼" from the block corners for seam allowance.

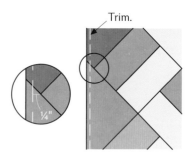

Trim.

¼"

## APPLIQUÉING THE LETTERS

**1.** Use the patterns below to trace the letters for *daddy's little girl* onto the paper side of fusible web, repeating letters as required. Roughly cut out the shapes and fuse to the wrong side of the remaining pink print, following the manufacturer's instructions. Cut out each appliqué along its outline and remove the paper backing.

**2.** Arrange the letters and apostrophe as shown along the right side of the quilt, in the open area created by the unpieced squares. Fuse the letters in place.

**3.** Use a machine blanket stitch to secure the edges of each appliqué to the quilt top.

## FINISHING THE QUILT

For more information on finishing techniques, go to ShopMartingale.com/HowtoQuilt for free illustrated instructions.

**1.** Layer the quilt top, batting, and backing, and baste the layers together. Quilt as desired.

**2.** Trim the backing and batting to match the quilt top.

**3.** Use the pink 2¼"-wide strips to bind the edges of the quilt. Add a label (if desired).

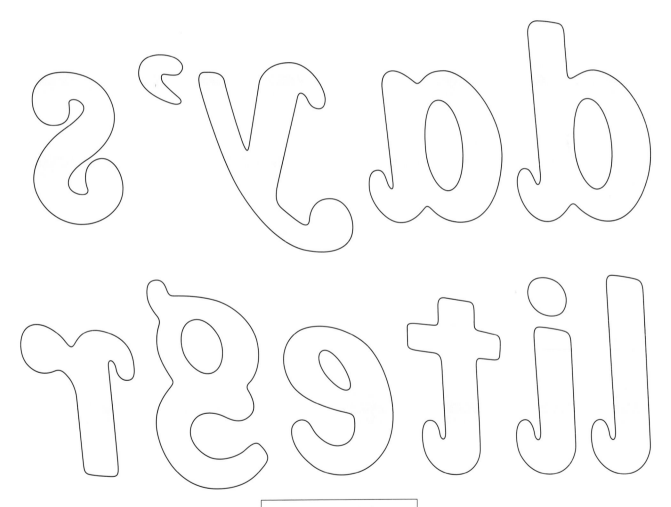

Patterns do not include seam allowances and are reversed for fusible appliqué.

# Fractured Hexagons

This baby quilt goes together quickly, and the result will always be unique—just like babies! From the placement, size, and colors of the hexagons to the one-of-a-kind fractures in the background, this graphic design is sure to please.

~Jen

## » Fabric Facts

Fabrics are from Tokyo Rocco by Carol Van Sandt for Andover Fabrics.

Varying hues and values in the background showcase the hexagon fabrics.

## MATERIALS

*Yardage is based on 42"-wide fabric.*

⅞ yard of medium-blue solid for background and binding

½ yard of gray solid for background

⅜ yard of white solid for background

⅓ yard of light-blue solid for background

25 to 30 scraps at least 5" x 5" (or charm squares) of assorted prints for hexagons

1½ yards of fabric for backing*

48" x 48" piece of batting

Template plastic or lightweight cardboard (optional)

Heavyweight paper for appliqués (optional)

Paper-backed fusible web (optional)

*\*The finished quilt size will vary from 40" to 44" in each dimension. Extra fabric is provided for the larger size possibilities, but it may be necessary to piece a backing panel from scraps.*

## » Bigger Backgrounds

For a quilt larger than 44" square, buy yardage equal to the desired quilt width, plus 10" to allow for the fractures. Cut the background strips lengthwise (parallel to the selvage) and join as many rows as you like.

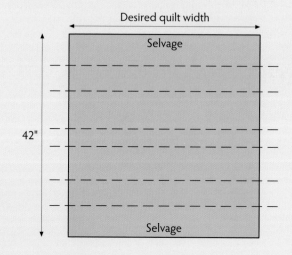

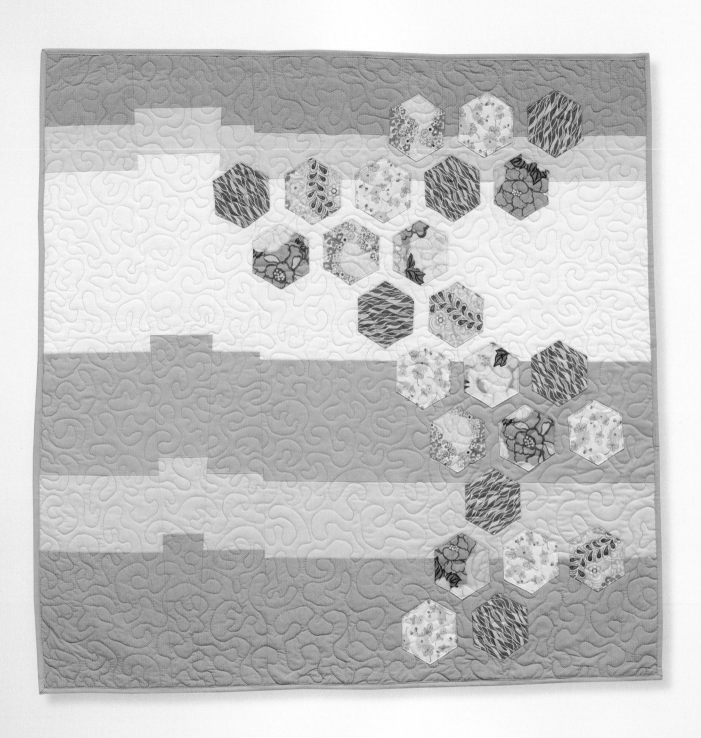

Designed and made by Jen Eskridge

## CUTTING

*Patterns are on page 29.*

*A ¼" seam allowance is included in all measurements unless otherwise specified. The background-strip widths and quantities can vary, but the goal is a combined width of 40" to 44" to make a square quilt.*

**From the medium-blue solid, cut:**
1 strip, 8½" x 42"
5 strips, 2¼" x 42"

**From the gray solid, cut:**
1 strip, 10½" x 42"
1 strip, 5½" x 42"

**From the white solid, cut:**
1 strip, 12½" x 42'

**From the light-blue solid, cut:**
1 strip, 5½" x 42"
1 strip, 3½" x 42"

> ### » Sizing Hexagons
>
> The hexagons can be any size from 3" to 5" in diameter. Incorporate a range of diameters for variety, or stick with a single size for a bold, graphic effect, as shown in the sample quilt. Use one or more of the patterns provided, or use the AccuQuilt Go! die-cutting system for quick hexagon cuts.

## PREPARING THE HEXAGONS

Choose traditional English paper piecing, line each shape with scrap fabric, or opt for speed with fusible web to prepare the hexagons for appliqué.

### ENGLISH PAPER PIECING

**1.** Trace the hexagon pattern or patterns of your choice onto the template material (lightweight cardboard or plastic). Use the template or templates to cut 25 to 30 hexagons from the assorted scraps or charm squares.

**2.** Remove the seam allowances from the hexagon template or templates. Use the modified template or templates to trace one hexagon on sturdy paper for each scrap-fabric hexagon.

**3.** Center a paper hexagon on the wrong side of a matching-size fabric hexagon. Fold the seam allowances over the paper shape and finger-press. Baste the seam allowances in place by hand, stitching through both fabric and paper. Repeat to prepare the desired number of scrap-fabric hexagons.

### LINED APPLIQUÉS

This technique requires additional fabric for the hexagon linings. Use scraps, or purchase muslin or cotton sheeting to use as the lining fabric.

**1.** Make a template from the hexagon pattern or patterns of your choice. Use the template or templates to cut a total of 25 to 30 hexagons from the assorted scrap fabrics and charm squares. Cut a lining for each hexagon, using the same hexagon template or templates. Pair each fabric hexagon with a lining hexagon, right sides together, and sew around all six edges.

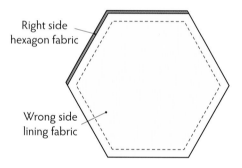

Right side
hexagon fabric

Wrong side
lining fabric

**2.** Trim the corners to remove bulk. Make a snip through the center of the lining fabric only, and turn the shape right side out through the opening. Press the shape, making sure the lining is completely concealed behind the finished fabric hexagon.

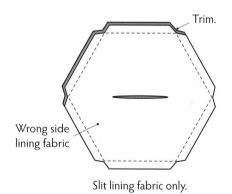

Trim.

Wrong side
lining fabric

Slit lining fabric only.

## FUSIBLE APPLIQUÉ

**1.** Trace the hexagon pattern or patterns of your choice, without seam allowances, onto fusible web, tracing a total of 25 to 30 hexagons. Roughly cut out each hexagon and fuse to the wrong side of each fabric scrap.

**2.** Cut out each hexagon along the traced outline. When the background is ready, follow the manufacturer's instructions to fuse the hexagons to the quilt top for a raw-edge appliqué appearance.

## BUILDING THE BACKGROUND

**1.** Join the background strips in the order shown or as desired. Press the seam allowances open to reduce bulk.

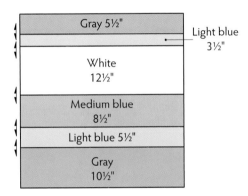

**2.** Fold one end of the assembled background at a slight angle with right sides together. Cut along the fold.

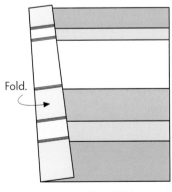

Cut along fold.

**3.** With the sections right sides together, slide the smaller piece down ½" to 1", keeping the cut edges aligned. Pin and restitch, using a ¼" seam

allowance. This creates the first fracture line. Press the seam allowances open.

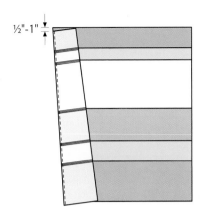

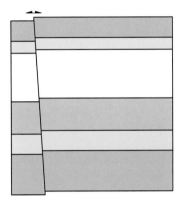

**4.** Repeat steps 2 and 3 to create three to five fracture seam lines in the quilt background. Vary the fold widths, angles, and slide directions to create a unique design.

**5.** Trim and square the background to the largest possible size. Although the sample quilt is square, trimming can yield either a square or a slightly rectangular shape.

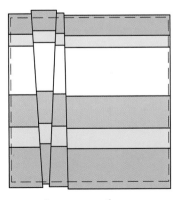

Square up quilt top.

## APPLYING THE HEXAGONS

**1.** Scatter the prepared hexagons on the background fabric. Ideally, the hexagons appear primarily on one half of the quilt, while the main fracture lines lie within the other half. Allow a few hexagons to overlap fracture lines, creating a unified, balanced piece.

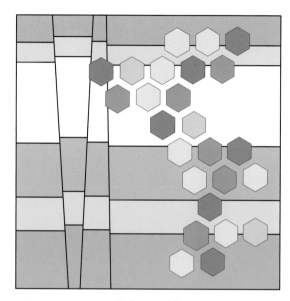

Quilt assembly

**2.** Once you have a general idea of where the hexagons will lie, position them more precisely, leaving 1" between shapes. Make sure each hexagon fabric contrasts against the adjacent background colors. Use two pins to hold each hexagon in place. If you are using fusible web, fuse the hexagons to the background.

**3.** Edgestitch each hexagon using a straight machine stitch.

### » Appliqué while Quilting

Consider using free-motion quilting to appliqué the hexagons and quilt the project all in one step.

## FINISHING THE QUILT

For more information on finishing techniques, go to ShopMartingale.com/HowtoQuilt for free illustrated instructions.

**1.** Layer the quilt top, batting, and backing, and baste the layers together. Quilt as desired.

**2.** Trim the backing and batting to match the quilt top.

**3.** Use the medium-blue 2¼"-wide strips to bind the edges of the quilt. Add a label (if desired).

### » Alternate Colorway

It's best to stick with solid colors for the background to keep the focus on the floating hexagons' prints.

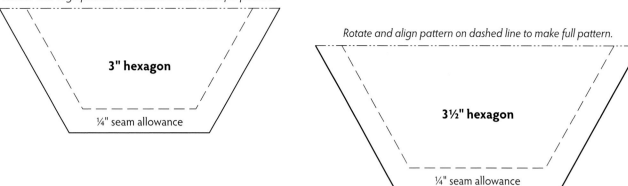

*Rotate and align pattern on dashed line to make full pattern.*

**3" hexagon**

¼" seam allowance

*Rotate and align pattern on dashed line to make full pattern.*

**3½" hexagon**

¼" seam allowance

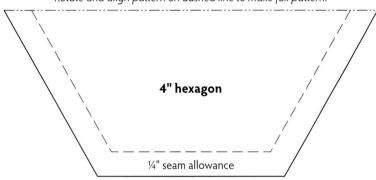

*Rotate and align pattern on dashed line to make full pattern.*

**4" hexagon**

¼" seam allowance

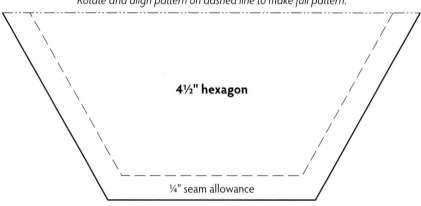

*Rotate and align pattern on dashed line to make full pattern.*

**4½" hexagon**

¼" seam allowance

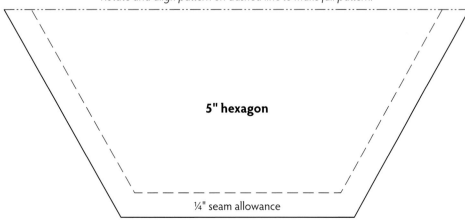

*Rotate and align pattern on dashed line to make full pattern.*

**5" hexagon**

¼" seam allowance

# Modern Shapes Sampler

**FINISHED QUILT: 36½" x 48½"  FINISHED BLOCK: 12" x 12"**

Shape sorters are a classic, beloved baby toy, and that nursery staple was the inspiration for this baby quilt. Strong, vibrant color and fussy-cut details combine with clean lines to make a quilt that little ones will love to explore.

~Sarah

### » Fabric Facts

You may wish to fussy cut some of the center patches to add interest. To include fussy-cut detail in the cross shape (the only block center not created from a single fabric piece), choose the fabric carefully and frame it in the long rectangular shape.

## MATERIALS

*Yardage is based on 42"-wide fabric except as noted. Some extra fabric is included for flexibility in construction.*

1 fat quarter *each* of 12 assorted fabrics for block backgrounds

¼ yard *OR* 1 scrap at least 8" x 8" *each* of 12 assorted prints for block centers

⅛ yard *each* of 12 nondirectional prints for block-center borders

⅜ yard of gray polka-dot fabric for binding

1½ yards of fabric for backing

42" x 54" piece of batting

Template plastic

## CUTTING

*A ¼" seam allowance is included in all measurements unless otherwise specified.*

*Organize the fabrics by block, selecting one fabric per block from each category: background, center, and border. You will make two blocks with each center shape, using different fabrics for every block.*

*Patterns are on pages 36–37. Trace each pattern onto template plastic and cut out; use the templates to cut fabric pieces as directed.*

### For *each* rectangle block, cut:

2 rectangles, 3½" x 8½", from the chosen background fabric
2 rectangles, 2½" x 12½", from the chosen background fabric
1 rectangle, 4½" x 6½", from the chosen center fabric
2 strips, 1½" x 4½", from the chosen border fabric
2 strips, 1½" x 8½", from the chosen border fabric

### For *each* square block, cut:

2 rectangles, 2½" x 8½", from the chosen background fabric
2 rectangles, 2½" x 12½", from the chosen background fabric
1 square, 6½" x 6½", from the chosen center fabric
2 strips, 1½" x 6½", from the chosen border fabric
2 strips, 1½" x 8½", from the chosen border fabric

*Continued on page 32*

Designed and made by Sarah Flynn

For *each* diamond block, cut:

2 squares, 8¾" x 8¾", from the chosen background fabric; cut in half diagonally to yield 4 triangles (two A and two B)

1 square, 4¾" x 4¾" (on point), from the chosen center fabric

2 strips, 1½" x 4¾", from the chosen border fabric

2 strips, 1½" x 6¾", from the chosen border fabric

For *each* triangle block, cut:

1 rectangle, 2¼" x 12½", from the chosen background fabric

2 rectangles, 7¾" x 11", from the chosen background fabric (C and D)*

1 triangle using pattern G from the chosen center fabric

1 strip, 1½" x 9½", from the chosen border fabric

1 strip, 1½" x 10", from the chosen border fabric

1 strip, 1½" x 10½", from the chosen border fabric

*See "Making the Blocks" to further cut these rectangles.*

For *each* hexagon block, cut:

2 rectangles, 2¾" x 12½", from the chosen background fabric

2 using pattern E from the chosen background fabric

2 using pattern F from the chosen background fabric

1 using pattern H from the chosen center fabric

6 strips, 1½" x 6½", from the chosen border fabric

For *each* cross block, cut:

4 squares, 4" x 4", from the chosen background fabric

4 rectangles, 2" x 5½", from the chosen background fabric

1 rectangle, 3½" x 7½", from the chosen center fabric

4 rectangles, 1½" x 3½", from the chosen center fabric

4 rectangles, 1½" x 2½", from the chosen border fabric

8 rectangles, 1½" x 3½", from the chosen border fabric

From the gray polka-dot fabric, cut:

5 strips, 2¼" x 42"

## MAKING THE BLOCKS

Make two of each block type. Press all seam allowances away from the block center.

### RECTANGLE BLOCK

**1.** Sew 1½" x 4½" border strips to the top and bottom of the block center. Sew a 1½" x 8½" border strip to each side.

**2.** Stitch a 3½" x 8½" background rectangle to each side of the center unit. Attach 2½" x 12½" background rectangles to the top and bottom to complete the block.

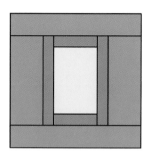

Rectangle block.
Make 2.

### SQUARE BLOCK

**1.** Sew 1½" x 6½" border strips to both sides of the block center. Add 1½" x 8½" border strips to the top and bottom.

**2.** Stitch 2½" x 8½" background rectangles to the top and bottom of the center unit. Sew 2½" x 12½" background rectangles to the block sides.

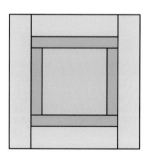

Square block.
Make 2.

### DIAMOND BLOCK

**1.** Sew 1½" x 4¾" border strips to opposite sides of the block center. Stitch 1½" x 6¾" border strips to the remaining sides.

**2.** Sew background triangles (A) to the upper-left and lower-right sides of the center unit, centering the triangles on the pieced center unit. Press the triangles away from the centers and trim the ends as shown.

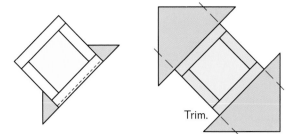

**3.** Sew the remaining background triangles (B) to the long sides of the pieced unit and press the triangles away from the center. Trim the block to 12½" x 12½".

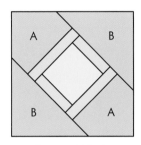

Diamond block.
Make 2.

### TRIANGLE BLOCK

**1.** Center the 1½" x 9½" border strip on the left edge of triangle piece G with right sides together. Sew, press, and trim the strip ends in line with the triangle edges, using a rotary cutter and ruler. Repeat to add the 1½" x 10" border strip to the right edge of the triangle and the 1½" x 10½" border strip to the bottom edge.

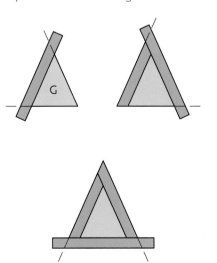

**2.** Lay one 7¾" x 11" rectangle right side up on a flat surface. Measure and mark a point on the lower edge, 2¾" from the bottom right corner. Draw a line connecting the mark with the upper left corner and cut along the line. The larger section is piece C; discard the smaller section. Repeat with the second 7¾" x 11" rectangle, but measure 2¾" from the bottom left corner and cut to the upper right corner. The larger piece created by this cut is piece D.

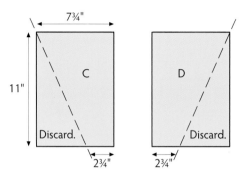

**3.** Sew piece C to the right side of the center unit. Align the seamlines at the lower edge of the center unit, allowing C to extend past the upper tip of the triangle. Press C away from the center unit and trim the upper edge of C in line with the edge of the center unit, as shown.

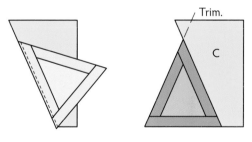

**4.** Stitch piece D to the left side. Measure the unit and trim to 12½" wide, centering the triangle.

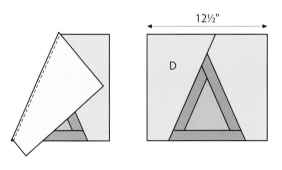

**5.** Add the 2¼" x 12½" background rectangle to the block's bottom edge. Trim the block to 12½" x 12½".

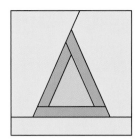

Triangle block.
Make 2.

## HEXAGON BLOCK

**1.** Center a 1½" x 6½" border strip on one side of hexagon piece H, right sides together, and stitch. Press the seam allowances outward and trim the excess strip in line with the raw edges of the hexagon, using a rotary cutter and ruler.

**2.** Working clockwise around the center hexagon, add the remaining border strips, trimming each strip to match the hexagon edges.

**3.** Sew E pieces to two opposite sides of the hexagon assembly. Match the F pieces to the long

edges of the unit and sew. Add 2¾" x 12½" background rectangles to the top and bottom edges.

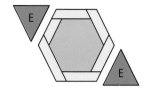 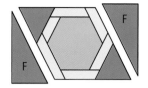

Press seam allowances outward.

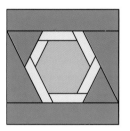

Hexagon block.
Make 2.

## CROSS BLOCK

**1.** Sew a 1½" x 3½" border rectangle to each end of the 3½" x 7½" center rectangle.

**2.** Sew a 1½" x 3½" border rectangle to each end of a 1½" x 3½" center rectangle. Make two. Stitch the pieced strips to the top and bottom edges of the unit from step 1.

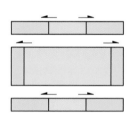 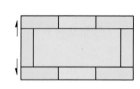

**3.** Sew 2" x 5½" background rectangles to the short ends of the assembled unit to complete the center row of the block.

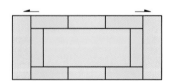

**4.** Sew a 1½" x 3½" center rectangle to a 1½" x 3½" border rectangle along one long edge. Stitch a 1½" x 2½" border rectangle to each short end of the unit. Make two.

**5.** Add a 2" x 5½" background rectangle to the border-fabric edge of the unit from step 4. Make two.

**6.** Sew a 4" background square to each end of the unit from step 5. Make two.

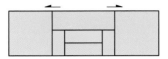

**7.** Stitch the units from step 6 to the top and bottom edges of the center row from step 3 to complete the block. Match the seams carefully and be sure the rows are oriented correctly to create the center cross.

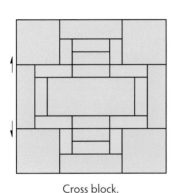

Cross block.
Make 2.

## ASSEMBLING THE QUILT TOP

Square up all blocks, as needed, to measure 12½" x 12½".

**1.** Arrange the blocks in four rows of three blocks each, creating a pleasing distribution of colors and shapes. The layout can vary, but to achieve a good balance no shape should appear twice in the same row or column.

**2.** Sew the blocks together into rows, pressing the seam allowances in alternating directions from row to row.

**3.** Sew the rows together. Press the seam allowances in one direction.

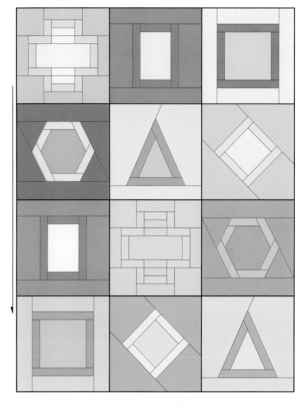

Quilt assembly

## FINISHING THE QUILT

For more information on finishing techniques, go to ShopMartingale.com/HowtoQuilt for free illustrated instructions.

**1.** Prepare the backing.

**2.** Layer the quilt top, batting, and backing, and baste the layers together. Quilt as desired.

**3.** Trim the backing and batting to match the quilt top.

**4.** Use the polka-dot 2¼"-wide strips to bind the edges of the quilt. Add a label (if desired).

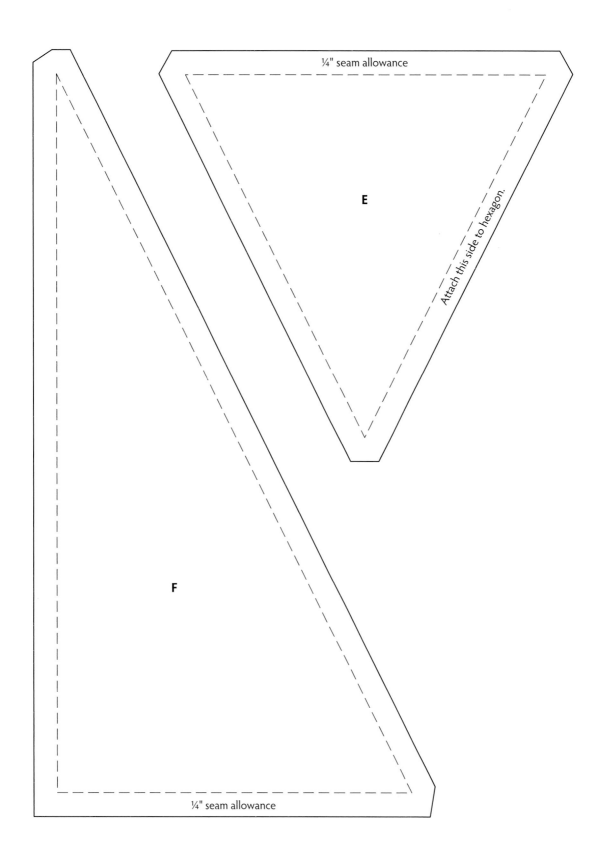

¼" seam allowance

E

Attach this side to hexagon.

F

¼" seam allowance

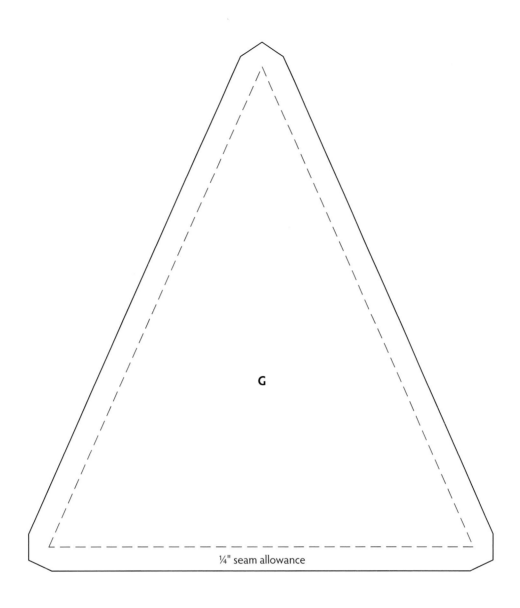

G

¼" seam allowance

*Rotate and align pattern on dashed line to make full pattern.*

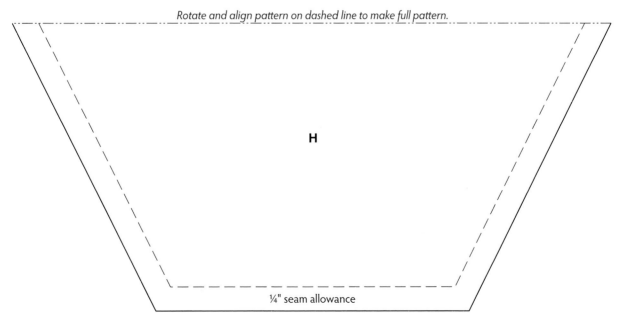

H

¼" seam allowance

# Bubbles

Dig into your scraps for this quirky and fun baby quilt. Different color choices for the background and the patchwork fish will completely transform the look.

~Dana

> **» Fabric Facts**
>
> This quilt is scrappy, but doesn't have to be. When choosing the fabrics, keep the small size of the appliqués in mind and select small-scale prints.

## MATERIALS

*Yardage is based on 42-wide fabric.*

1 yard of pale-aqua solid for background

15 scraps at least 5" x 5" of assorted blue fabrics for bubbles

11 scraps at least 1½" x 7" of assorted orange fabrics for fish

⅜ yard of orange print for binding

1⅜ yards of fabric for backing

42" x 48" piece of batting

Template plastic

## CUTTING

*A ¼" seam allowance is included in all measurements unless otherwise specified.*

*Patterns are on page 41. Trace the patterns onto template plastic and cut out; use the templates to cut fabric pieces as directed. Do not add seam allowances to these raw-edge appliqué pieces.*

**From the assorted blue fabrics, cut:**

3 using pattern A

7 using pattern B

5 using pattern C

**From the assorted orange fabrics, cut:**

11 rectangles, 1½" x 7"

**From the orange print, cut:**

5 strips, 2¼" x 42"

## ASSEMBLING THE QUILT TOP

**1.** Sew the 11 orange rectangles together along the long edges. Press the seam allowances in one direction.

**2.** Using the fish pattern on page 41, trace and cut one fish shape from the strip set.

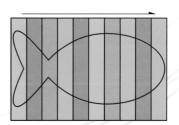

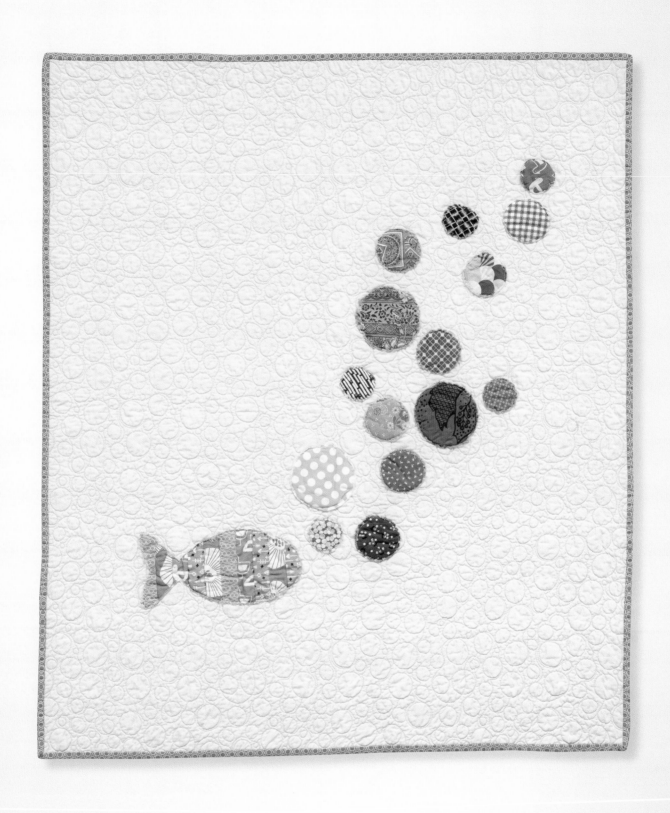

Designed and pieced by Dana Bolyard; machine quilted by Russ Adams of the Back Porch Quilters

## » Hold Steady

Starch is your friend! Using a quality spray starch on the orange strip set will not only yield straighter strips, but also provide more body and stability as you cut out the fish shape.

**3.** Press the aqua background fabric to remove wrinkles and creases.

**4.** Pin the strip-pieced fish to the background fabric about 5½" from the left side and 8½" above the bottom edge.

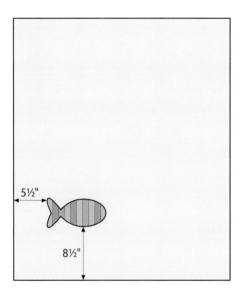

**5.** Using either a short straight stitch or a zigzag stitch on your machine, sew ⅛" inside the raw edges of the fish. Backtack at the beginning and end.

## » Appliqué Tips

- Use lots of pins on the appliqués; the more pins, the better!
- Remove the pins as you sew around the appliqué shape.
- Always be sure the appliqué and background fabrics are smooth, straight, and correctly positioned.
- Slip a layer of tear-away stabilizer under the background fabric, if desired.

**6.** Position the bubbles on the background fabric, using the diagram below and the quilt photo on page 39 for placement suggestions. Attach the bubbles in the same manner as the fish appliqué.

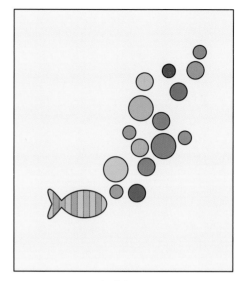

Quilt layout

## FINISHING THE QUILT

For more information on finishing techniques, go to ShopMartingale.com/HowtoQuilt for free illustrated instructions.

**1.** Prepare the backing.

**2.** Layer the quilt top, batting, and backing, and baste the layers together. Quilt as desired. The sample quilt features a continuous-line quilting pattern of small circles that echo the appliquéd bubbles.

**3.** Trim the backing and batting to match the quilt top.

**4.** Use the orange 2¼"-wide strips to bind the edges of the quilt. Add a label (if desired).

**5.** Wash the finished quilt to remove all starch residue and to fray the edges of the appliqués.

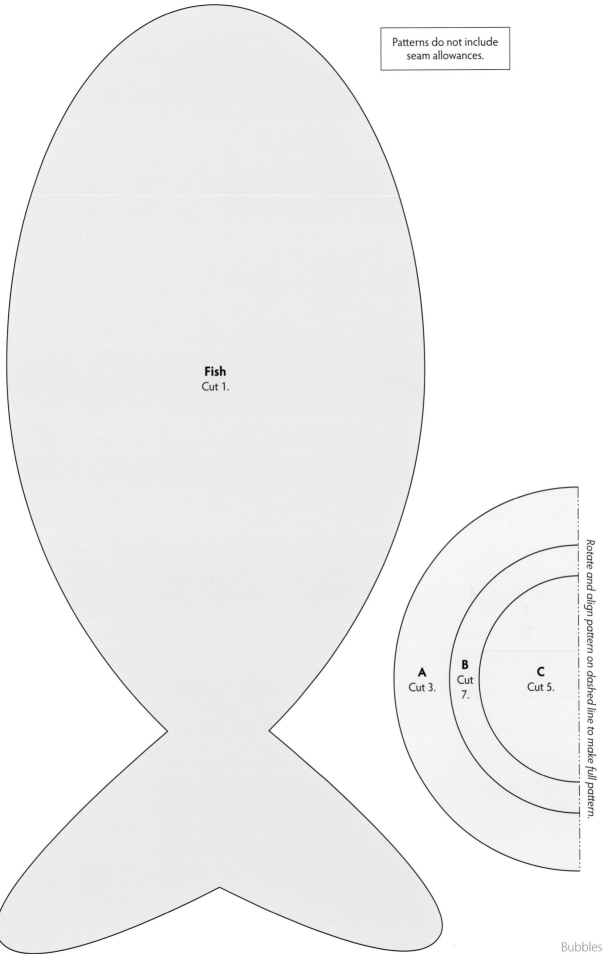

Patterns do not include seam allowances.

**Fish**
Cut 1.

**A**
Cut 3.

**B**
Cut 7.

**C**
Cut 5.

Rotate and align pattern on dashed line to make full pattern.

# Cross Weave

I love how "modern" quilts can come from very traditional blocks. I also enjoy the look of a mono-chromatic, but scrappy, quilt. It's a fun way to play with visual textures and shades rather than color contrast. This simple pattern creates a visually stimulating design for babies. The pattern works well with assorted 5" charm squares and 2½"-wide Jelly Roll strips.

~ Amy

> **» Fabric Facts**
>
> This quilt is great for using a variety of monochromatic scraps. Choose lots of different patterns and shades from the same color family, and add a contrasting solid (white in the sample) to unify the quilt. The result is visually interesting and quick to make.

## MATERIALS

*Yardage is based on 42"-wide fabric.*

1⅜ yards of white solid for blocks and outer border

5" x 5" square *each* of 21 assorted red or pink prints for blocks

2½" x 42" strip *each* of 6 or more assorted red or pink prints for blocks

⅝ yard of dotted pink fabric for inner border and binding

2⅝ yards of fabric for backing

47" x 52" piece of batting

## CUTTING

*A ¼" seam allowance is included in all measurements.*

### From the white solid, cut:
3 strips, 5" x 42"; crosscut into 21 squares, 5" x 5". Cut once diagonally to yield 42 triangles.

6 strips, 2½" x 42"; crosscut into 21 rectangles, 2½" x 9"

4 strips, 3½" x 42"; crosscut into 2 rectangles, 3½" x 41", and 2 rectangles, 3½" x 41½"*

### From the assorted-print strips, cut *a total of:*
21 rectangles, 2½" x 9"

### From the dotted pink fabric, cut:
2 strips, 1½" x 39"
2 strips, 1½" x 35½"
5 strips, 2¼" x 42"

*\* Cut a 5th strip and piece the borders, if necessary.*

## MAKING THE BLOCKS

**1.** Fold a white triangle in half and finger-press the long edge at the fold to create a center point. Repeat with a second white triangle. Fold a 2½" x 9" print rectangle in half and finger-press the long edges at the fold. Sew the white triangles to opposite

Designed and made by Amy Smart

sides of the rectangle, aligning the center points. Press the seam allowances toward the rectangle.

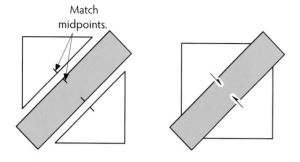

Match midpoints.

**2.** Square and trim each block to 6" x 6". Make 21.

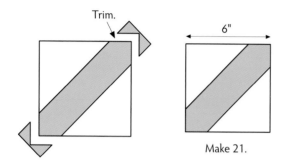

Trim.

6"

Make 21.

**3.** Cut each assorted red- or pink-print square once diagonally to create 2 triangles (42 total). Repeat steps 1 and 2, pairing assorted-print triangles with white rectangles. Press the seam allowances toward the print triangles. Make 21.

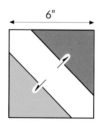

6"

Make 21.

## ASSEMBLING THE QUILT TOP

**1.** Arrange the blocks in seven rows of six blocks each, alternating white-triangle blocks and print-triangle blocks.

**2.** Sew the blocks together into rows, pressing seam allowances in alternating directions from row to row.

**3.** Sew the rows together. Press the seam allowances in one direction.

**4.** Stitch a pink 1½" x 39" inner-border strip to each side of the quilt top. Press the seam allowances toward the border strips. Add the pink 1½" x 35½" strips to the top and bottom edges. Press the seam allowances toward the border strips.

**5.** Sew a white 3½" x 41" outer-border strip to each side of the quilt top. Add the white 3½" x 41½" strips to the top and bottom edges. Press the seam allowances toward the outer borders.

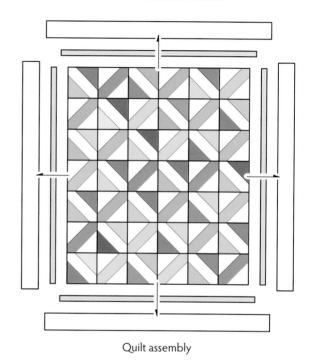

Quilt assembly

## FINISHING THE QUILT

For more information on finishing techniques, go to ShopMartingale.com/HowtoQuilt for free illustrated instructions.

**1.** Prepare the backing fabric.

**2.** Layer the quilt top, batting, and backing, and baste the layers together. Quilt as desired.

**3.** Trim the backing and batting to match the quilt top.

**4.** Use the pink 2¼"-wide strips to bind the edges of the quilt. Add a label (if desired).

# The Birdhouse Quilt

**FINISHED QUILT: 36½" x 49"**

This artful quilt is delightfully easy to create using simple fusible-appliqué techniques. Have fun choosing scraps for your oversized flower garden and whimsical rooftop bird. Playful, overlapping free-motion stitches and simple cutout shapes give this quilt a hand-drawn and collaged feeling.

~ Carrie

## »Fabric Facts

- If you prefer, use a variety of green fabric scraps to piece a rectangle large enough for the strip of grass in the quilt background.

- Let your garden speak about you! Showcase quirky fabrics and use them as a painter would use paints. To see the composition more clearly before permanently fusing the appliqués to the background, use one of my painter's tricks: Stand back and squint. This helps you see color value more clearly and makes it obvious which fabrics are too bold or too muted.

## MATERIALS

*Yardage is based on 42"-wide fabric.*

1¼ yards of cream fabric for background
⅜ yard of yellow-green streaked print for grass
15" x 26" piece of dotted turquoise fabric for house
7" x 13" or larger piece of green print for grass
3" x 12" piece of green print for stems and leaves
3" x 12" piece of light-brown print for stems and twig
Assorted small scraps for windows, door, flowers, and bird
½ yard of polka-dot fabric for binding
1½ yards of fabric for backing
42" x 55" piece of batting
Tracing paper
Lightweight fusible web
Contrasting thread for appliqué

## CUTTING

*A ¼" seam allowance is included in all measurements unless otherwise specified.*

**From the cream fabric, cut:**
1 square, 36½" x 36½"

**From the yellow-green streaked print, cut:**
1 rectangle, 13" x 30"

**From the dotted turquoise fabric, cut:**
1 rectangle, 15" x 26"

**From the green print for grass, cut:**
1 rectangle, 7" x 13"

**From the polka-dot fabric, cut:**
5 strips, 2¼" x 42"

## PREPARING THE APPLIQUÉS

The quilt top is created with fusible appliqué. The process is very direct and simple—similar to making a cut-and-paste collage. There is no right or wrong way to interpret the design. If you want more or fewer flowers or windows, go for it!

Designed and sewn by Carrie Bloomston; quilted by Mary Beth Martin

**1.** Using a pencil and the patterns on pages 49–53, trace the pieces for the windows, flowers, bird, and twig onto the paper side of fusible web. You will make the leaves later. The patterns have already been reversed for tracing. Enlarge the house, door, door edge, and door opening patterns as indicated and trace them onto fusible web. Label each piece as you trace so that you can keep track of all the appliqués.

**2.** Roughly cut around each shape. Place the fusible web on the wrong side of your fabric selections and fuse each shape in place, following the manufacturer's instructions. Cut out each shape along the traced outline. Do not cut out the windows in the house appliqué; those lines are guides for placement only.

**» Keep It Organized**

Leave the labeled paper on the fusible web until just before you appliqué the piece to the quilt. You may prefer to cut out the small shapes a few at a time as the project calls for them, leaving less chance of mixing them up or losing a tiny appliqué piece.

## APPLIQUÉING THE HOUSE

**1.** With the backing paper still intact on the large house appliqué, remove the paper from the windows and door opening and position them on the right side of the house fabric. (Don't add the door yet.) Fuse the pieces to the house.

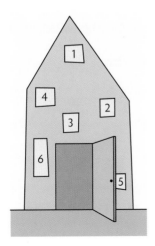

**» Perfect Placement**

To make a placement guide for the house details, trace the house pattern onto tracing paper and flip it over. Place the tracing-paper template on top of the house appliqué and slip each window and the door rectangle into position.

**2.** Remove the paper backing from the house and position it on the cream background square, using the quilt photo on page 46 as a placement guide. Match the bottom raw edge of the house to the bottom edge of the background, with the lower-right corner of the house 6" from the background's right edge. Fuse the house in place.

## PIECING THE GRASS

**1.** Pin the green-print rectangle to the yellow-green rectangle, right sides together, along the 13" edge. Sew them together and press the seam allowances open.

**2.** Stitch the grass unit to the lower edge of the background/house piece, right sides together, catching the lower edge of the house appliqué in the seam. Press the seam allowances toward the grass.

## APPLIQUÉING THE GARDEN

**1.** Position the door along the right edge of the door opening. The door and opening will align at their corners, with the bottom of the door overlapping the grass. Add the tiny door edge to the right edge of the door, overlapping it slightly, and fuse in place.

**2.** Position the flowers on the background as shown or as desired and pin or baste. Have fun with this! There is no wrong way. You can make a garden exactly like the one shown, or add or remove flowers. In designer Carrie's words, *"Celebrate your inner artist!"*

**3.** Cut two 3" x 12" rectangles of fusible web and apply one to the wrong side of each green and light-brown stem and leaf fabric. Using a rotary cutter, freehand cut stem strips about ⅛" wide; the strip heights can be adjusted later. Vary the stems to look artful and natural.

**4.** Position a stem with each flower, tucking the stem's upper end under the flower where they meet. Allow the stems to extend onto the grass to varying lengths, trimming the stems as necessary.

**5.** Trace leaf pieces A–E onto the paper side of fusible web and cut them out, reserving them for the final appliqué section. Using fusible-web-backed scraps of the green fabric and the leaf patterns on page 50, cut a few tiny leaves and position them on the flower stems. When the placement of the stems, small leaves, and flowers is satisfactory, fuse everything in place. Voilà! An artful garden.

## STITCHING THE APPLIQUÉS

**1.** Set your sewing machine for a free-motion stitch by lowering or covering the feed dogs and attaching a darning or free-motion foot. See your machine's manual for specific instructions. If you're uncomfortable with free-motion stitching, use a regular straight stitch, sew slowly, and overlap the lines of stitching. Thread the needle with a contrasting thread for a sketched appearance; the sample quilt uses shades of gray.

**2.** Stitch around the perimeter of each shape in a loopy, hand-drawn way, sewing around each shape multiple times for an artful look. Although the quilt uses fusible web, it is important to sew around each edge to lock it in place and help prevent fraying.

**3.** Add details such as flower petals and feathers with free-motion embroidery as shown.

## APPLIQUÉING THE BIRD AND TWIG

**1.** Position the bird body near the rooftop as shown. Tuck the beak and tail under the body and lay the wing on top. Slip the twig under the beak and add the remaining leaves beside the twig or tucked under its edges. Fuse all the pieces in place.

**2.** Use a straight machine stitch and contrasting thread to stitch the bird's legs on the background. Create the bird's eye with a French knot, a tiny fabric scrap, or free-motion stitches.

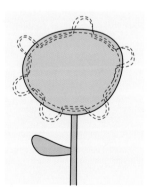

**4.** Stitch the windowpanes along the dashed lines on the patterns, stitching each line several times. In the sample quilt, smaller windowpane squares were layered over the window appliqués after they were stitched; this step is optional. To create the layered effect, cut little squares from a coordinating fabric backed with fusible web, using the stitched panes as guides. Fuse the contrasting panes in place and attach them with matching thread.

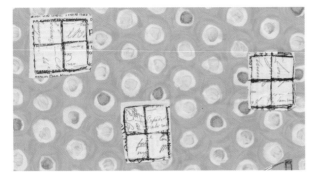

*Create a layered look by adding windowpanes of coordinating fabric, if desired.*

## FINISHING THE QUILT

For more information on finishing techniques, go to ShopMartingale.com/HowtoQuilt for free illustrated instructions.

**1.** Prepare the backing.

**2.** Layer the quilt top, batting, and backing, and baste the layers together. Quilt as desired.

**3.** Trim the backing and batting to match the quilt top.

**4.** Use the polka-dot 2¼"-wide strips to bind the edges of the quilt. Add a label (if desired).

> Patterns do not include seam allowances and are reversed for fusible appliqué.

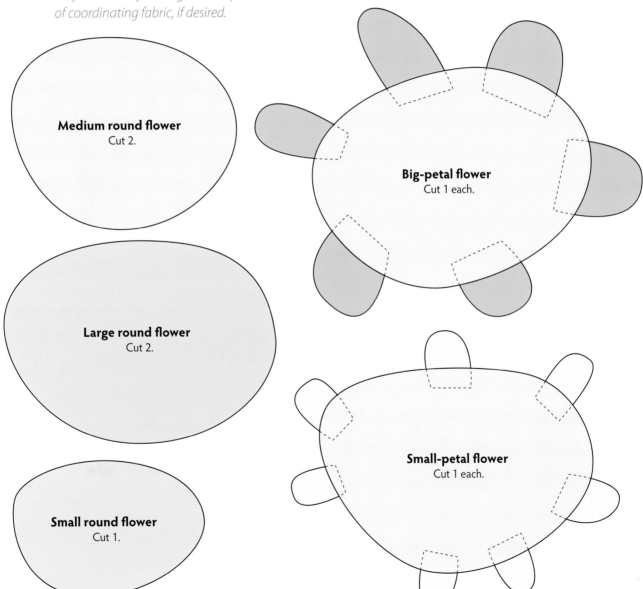

**Medium round flower**
Cut 2.

**Large round flower**
Cut 2.

**Small round flower**
Cut 1.

**Big-petal flower**
Cut 1 each.

**Small-petal flower**
Cut 1 each.

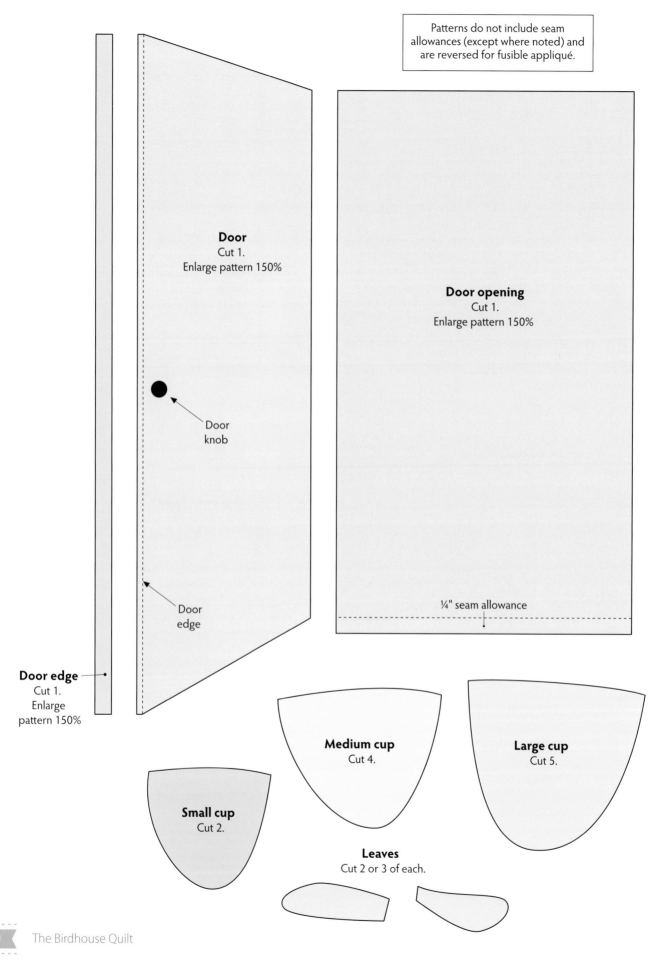

Patterns do not include seam allowances (except where noted) and are reversed for fusible appliqué.

**Door**
Cut 1.
Enlarge pattern 150%

**Door opening**
Cut 1.
Enlarge pattern 150%

Door knob

Door edge

¼" seam allowance

**Door edge**
Cut 1.
Enlarge pattern 150%

**Medium cup**
Cut 4.

**Large cup**
Cut 5.

**Small cup**
Cut 2.

**Leaves**
Cut 2 or 3 of each.

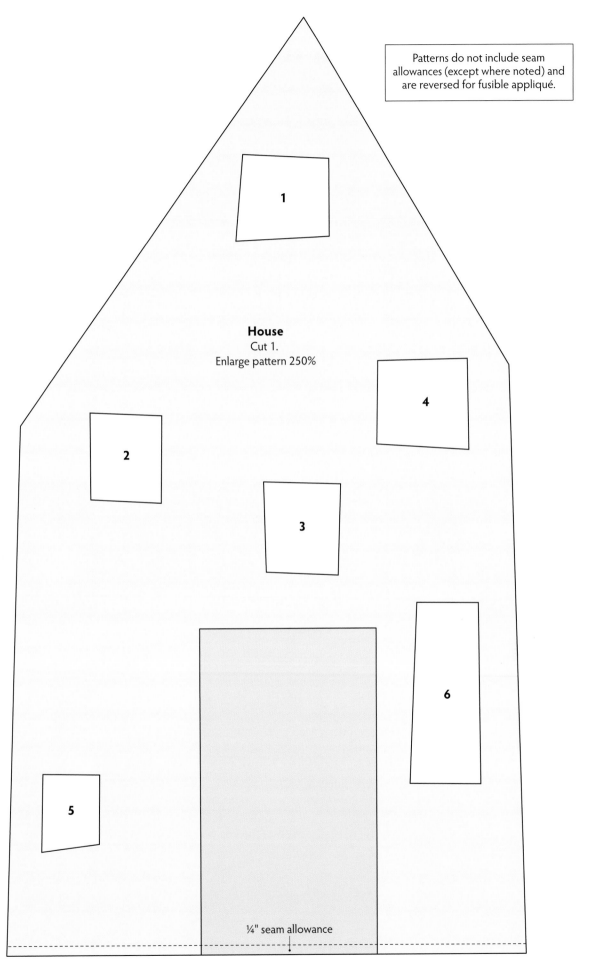

Patterns do not include seam allowances (except where noted) and are reversed for fusible appliqué.

**House**
Cut 1.
Enlarge pattern 250%

1

4

2

3

6

5

¼" seam allowance

## Windows
Cut 1 each.

1

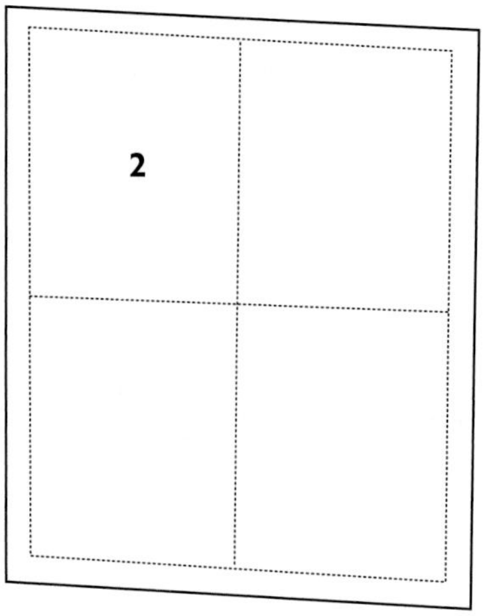

2

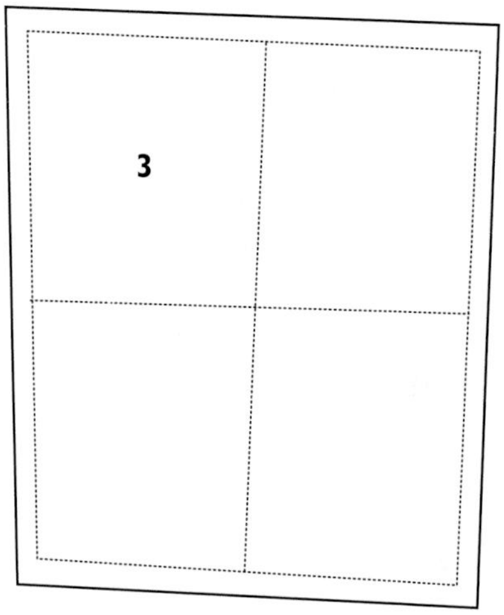

3

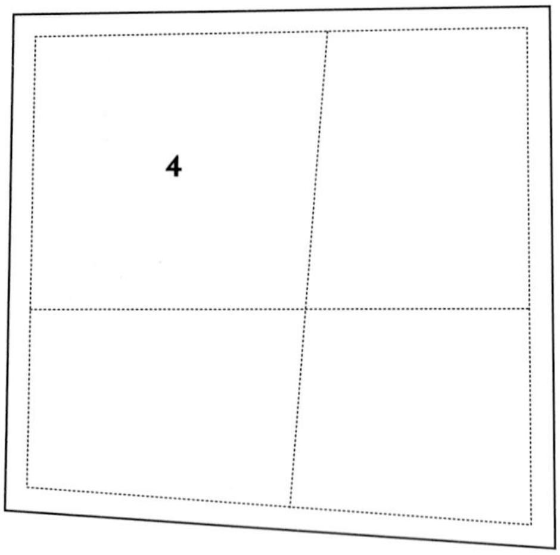

4

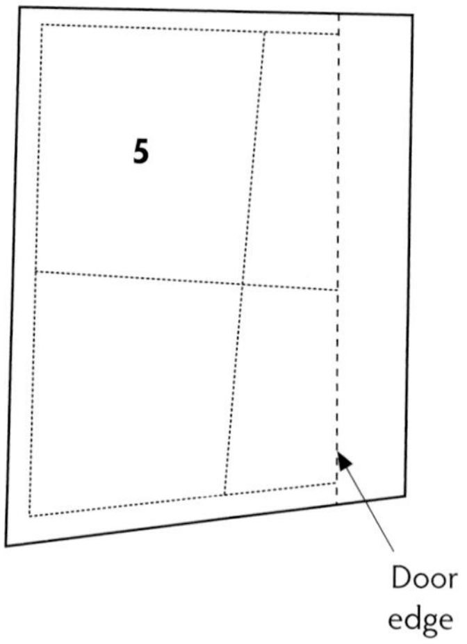

5

Door
edge

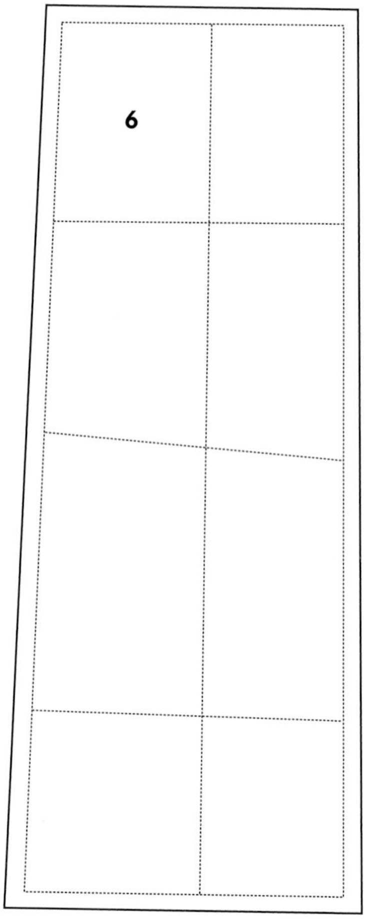

6

------------ Indicates stitching line

Patterns on this page are full
sized. Patterns do not include
seam allowances and are
reversed for fusible appliqué.

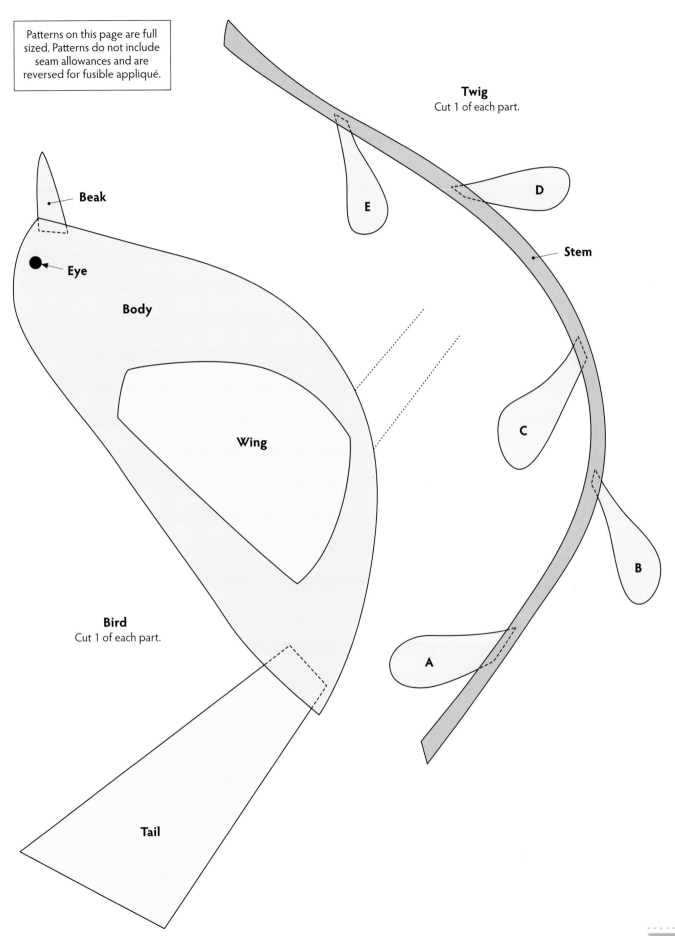

Patterns on this page are full sized. Patterns do not include seam allowances and are reversed for fusible appliqué.

**Twig**
Cut 1 of each part.

E

D

**Stem**

**Beak**

**Eye**

**Body**

C

**Wing**

B

**Bird**
Cut 1 of each part.

A

**Tail**

# Marbles

Make a modern baby quilt that's fast, simple, and offers something extra. I hand embroidered each circle and outlined my 11-year-old daughter's hands in the corner, as if a child were dropping marbles. Add a baby's name and birth information to the quilt's open space, or appliqué solid-color marbles on a print background for a different twist. Challenge yourself to make it your own!

~Jake

> ## » Fabric Facts
>
> Fabrics in the sample quilt include Robert Kaufman Essex cotton/linen blend (background); Robert Kaufman Kona Cotton (black); Cherrywood solids (large circles); and Michael Miller Fabrics Fairy Frost (small circles). The fusible web is Steam-A-Seam 2 Lite.

## MATERIALS

*Yardage is based on 42"-wide fabric.*

1½ yards of white solid for background

1 yard of black solid for medium circles and binding

16 squares, 5" x 5", of assorted solid colors (or charm squares) for large circles

16 squares, 5" x 5", of assorted solid colors (or charm squares) for small circles

2¼ yards of fabric for backing*

46" x 46" piece of batting

Lightweight fusible web

Black pearl cotton, size 8

Template plastic

*\*If your backing fabric is 4" to 6" wider than the quilt top, you may be able to cut a single length for the backing. In this case, you will need just 1½ yards of backing fabric.*

## CUTTING

*A ¼" seam allowance is included in all measurements unless otherwise specified.*

### From the white solid, cut:
1 square, 41" x 41"

### From the black solid, cut:
4 strips, 8" x 42"
Reserve the remaining black fabric for appliqués.

## PREPARING THE QUILT LAYERS

To create the impression that the circles are sitting on top of the quilt, the quilt layers are stacked and quilted before the circles are appliquéd.

**1.** Prepare the backing fabric. Layer the white background square, batting, and backing, and baste the layers together.

**2.** Quilt the entire surface as desired.

Designed and made by Jake Finch

## PREPARING THE CIRCLES

**1.** Using a permanent marker and the patterns on page 58, trace the three circles onto template plastic. Cut them out on the lines. Use the templates to trace 16 circles of each size (48 total) onto the paper side of the fusible web. Leave at least ¼" between circles. Roughly cut out each circle.

**2.** Following the manufacturer's instructions, fuse a large or small circle to the wrong side of each 5" fabric square. Fuse the medium circles to the wrong side of the black solid. Carefully cut out each circle on its traced outline. No seam allowance is necessary for fused appliqués.

**3.** Arrange the circles in 16 groups, each containing a small, medium, and large circle.

**4.** Remove the paper backing from the black circle in one group and position it on the large circle, about ⅛" from the large circle's raw edge. Remove the paper from the small circle and position it on the black circle, this time leaving a ¹⁄₁₆" margin for stitching. Leave the backing in place on the large circle so that it doesn't stick to your ironing board, or use a nonstick pressing sheet if you wish. Fuse the circles together. Make 16.

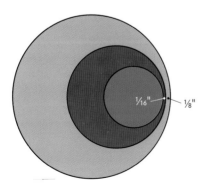

Make 16.

**5.** Remove the backing paper from the large circles and lay out the prepared units across the quilt top, using the diagram as a guide. Leave at least 2" of space along the quilt edges to allow for trimming and binding. Fuse the circle units to the quilt.

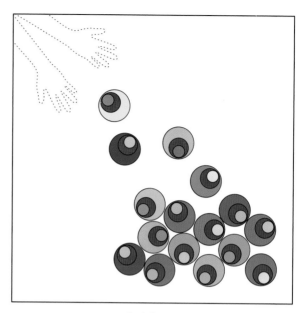

Quilt layout

## BINDING THE QUILT

An extra-wide binding, 1½" wide, serves as a bold frame for this simple quilt.

**1.** Trim the quilt to 40" x 40".

**2.** Sew the black binding strips together along their short ends to make one continuous length. Fold the strip in half lengthwise with wrong sides together and press.

**3.** Align the binding and quilt raw edges and sew the binding to the quilt with a 1½" seam allowance. Miter each corner. Join the ends of the binding and finish stitching it in place. For more information, go to ShopMartingale.com/HowtoQuilt for free illustrated instructions.

**4.** Fold the binding to the quilt's wrong side, pressing the corners carefully. Slip-stitch the binding fold to the quilt back, just covering the seam line.

## STITCHING THE APPLIQUÉS AND EMBROIDERY

**1.** Thread a crewel or embroidery needle with one strand of size 8 pearl cotton. Sew each circle to the quilt through all layers with a running stitch placed about ⅛" from the circle's raw edge. If desired, appliqué the circles by machine instead. Use a satin, zigzag, or straight stitch, or experiment with decorative stitches and contrasting threads. Keep in mind that wider stitches work best on the large circles.

> ### » A Little Protection
>
> A thimble is a must for stitching through the multiple layers of appliqué and quilt by hand!

**2.** Trace the hand pattern on page 58 onto template plastic and cut out. Using a removable marker, trace two hands in the upper-left corner of the quilt top, reversing the template for the second hand. Stitch along the hand outlines with a running stitch and size 8 pearl cotton, or machine stitch if desired. As the final touch, add a label to your quilt.

> ### » Remember This
>
> Create a memory quilt for a baby shower or other special occasion by asking guests and loved ones to sign the circles with a permanent fabric marker.

> ### » Quilting Ideas
>
> The free-motion quilting shown consists simply of circles looping across the quilt, but this quilt's open design allows for many other playful choices. Consider "writing" names and dates with contrasting thread or using more graphic designs. Have fun with your quilting, and your quilt will benefit!

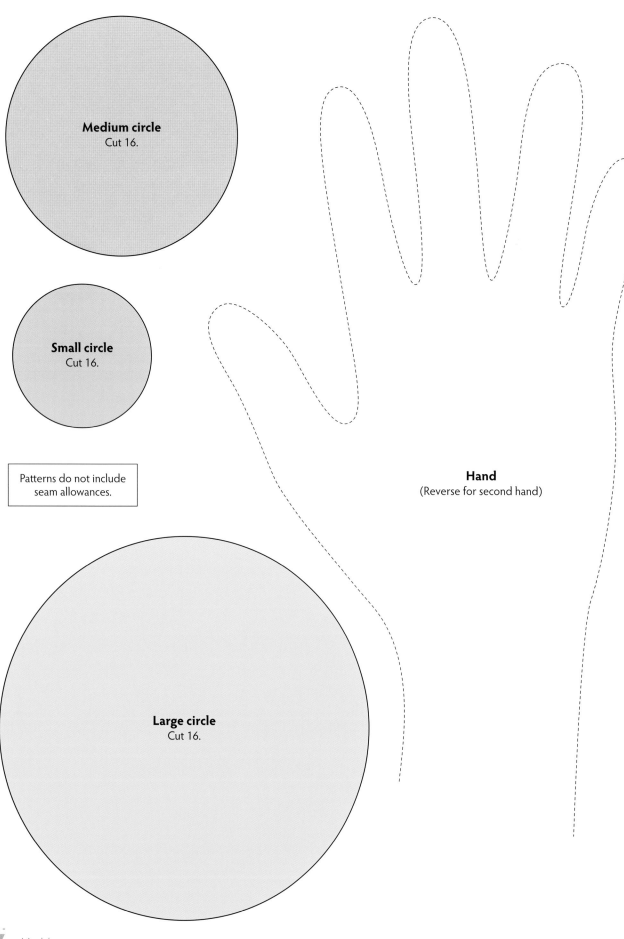

**Medium circle**
Cut 16.

**Small circle**
Cut 16.

Patterns do not include
seam allowances.

**Large circle**
Cut 16.

**Hand**
(Reverse for second hand)

# Vertigo

You'll fall head over heels for this dizzyingly bright, playful quilt. I used two different values of a single color in each vertical strip, creating a mesmerizing optical effect that adds to the fun!

~Audrie

## » Fabric Facts

Quilt fabrics are Robert Kaufman Kona Cotton Solids (Black, Pepper, Coal, Gold, Yarrow, Curry, Corn Yellow, Canary, Maize, Teal Blue, Caribbean, Lagoon, Robin Egg, Aqua, Moss, Olive, Hibiscus, Mulberry, Magenta, Violet, Pansy, and Thistle) and Moda Bella Solids (Steel, Silver, Feather, Turquoise, Terrain Cactus, Curry, Light Lime, and Chartreuse).

## MATERIALS

*Yardage is based on 42"-wide fabric except as noted. This quilt is made using 5 color groups, each containing 6 different shades of a single color. Fat eighths measure 9" x 21", but scraps at least 7" x 13" will also work.*

1 fat eighth *each* of 6 assorted purple solids
1 fat eighth *each* of 6 assorted teal solids
1 fat eighth *each* of 6 assorted green solids
1 fat eighth *each* of 6 assorted yellow solids
1 fat eighth *each* of 6 assorted gray solids
⅜ yard of gray print for binding
2⅜ yards of fabric for backing
47" x 48" piece of batting

## CUTTING

*A ¼" seam allowance is included in all measurements.*

### From *each* of the fat eighths, cut:

1 rectangle, 7" x 13"; crosscut into 4 strips, various widths x 13" (120 total)*

### From the binding fabric, cut:

5 strips, 2¼" x 42"

*\*Be sure to cut each strip a slightly different width; it's OK if the cuts are slightly skewed, but don't make them too wonky or you may encounter problems when trying to assemble the quilt top. The four strips should have a combined width of 7".*

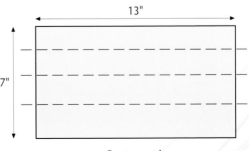

Cutting guide

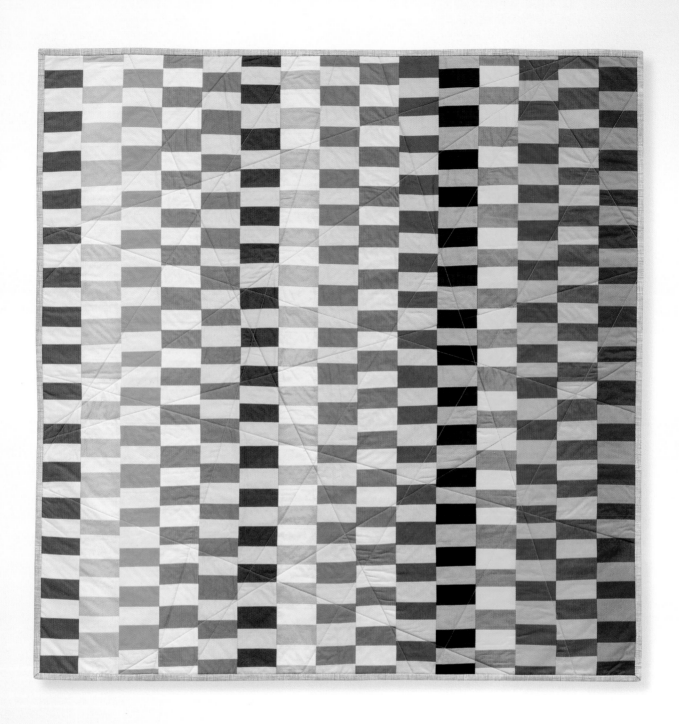

Designed and made by Audrie Bidwell

## MAKING THE STRIP SETS

**1.** Stack the strips from each of the 30 fabrics separately. Within each color group, arrange the strips from light to dark and label the stacks from A (lightest) to F (darkest).

**2.** Pair the strips within each color grouping as follows: A and D, B and E, C and F. Sew the strips together in pairs, randomizing the strip widths. Join matching pairs to create one strip set for each color/value pairing. Press the seam allowances to one side. Make 3 strip sets from each color group, for a total of 15.

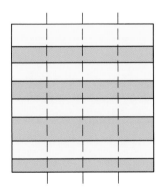

Make 3 strip sets of each color group;
15 total.

**3.** Square up the strip sets by trimming all edges with a rotary cutter and ruler. Cut each strip set into four sections of equal width, which can range from 2½" to 3" depending on the finished width of your strip sets. For example, if the strip set is 12" wide, cut each section 3" wide.

Cut 4 equal-width sections.

## ASSEMBLING THE QUILT TOP

**1.** Sew four matching pieced segments end to end. Press the seam allowances in one direction.

Repeat for each set of matching strips to make 15 two-color columns. Trim the columns to the same length.

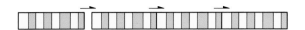

**2.** Arrange the strips on your design wall. In the quilt shown, Audrie arranged her strips from light to dark, working through the color sequence gray, yellow, teal, green, and purple three times. To achieve the quilt's optical effect, the tops of the columns must alternate between dark and light values. Rotate columns as necessary to achieve correct value placement.

Quilt assembly

**3.** Sew the columns together and press the seam allowances open to avoid bulk.

## FINISHING THE QUILT

For more information on finishing techniques, go to ShopMartingale.com/HowtoQuilt for free illustrated instructions.

**1.** Prepare the backing.

**2.** Layer the quilt top, batting, and backing, and baste the layers together. Quilt as desired.

**3.** Trim the backing and batting to match the quilt top.

**4.** Use the gray 2¼"-wide strips to bind the edges of the quilt. Add a label (if desired).

# Star Light, Star Bright

**FINISHED QUILT: 56½" x 56½" FINISHED BLOCK: 18" x 18"**

This baby quilt is inspired by those old, much-laundered, deeply loved star quilts that fade gracefully with age, losing parts of stars into the background as their colors wash away. To make that well-worn white work effectively in a modern quilt, I chose prints containing white and combined them with three solids—light, medium, and dark—to create movement. Embroidered star outlines are the crowning touch as the pattern blends into the background.

~ Victoria

> ## » Fabric Facts
>
> Victoria chose a selection of aqua, turquoise, and royal-blue solid fabrics. She used a wool batting, but you can opt for cotton or another fiber if you prefer.

## MATERIALS

*Yardage is based on 42"-wide fabric.*

4 yards of white solid for blocks and background
¼ yard *each* of 8 to 10 assorted blue-and-white prints for blocks
¼ yard *each* of 3 assorted blue solids for blocks
½ yard of blue print for binding
3½ yards of fabric for backing
62" x 62" piece of batting
Variegated blue pearl cotton, size 8
Template plastic

> ## » Finding Fabrics
>
> Focus on selecting prints that contain a lot of white, and that represent a range from light to dark. Prints that are primarily white will seem white, while a navy-blue crosshatch print with only bits of white will read darker. Laying out your pieces on a design wall will help you arrange them for the most appealing effect.

## CUTTING

*A ¼" seam allowance is included in all measurements unless otherwise specified.*

From the *lengthwise grain* of the white solid, cut:
2 strips, 11½" x 36½"
2 strips, 11½" x 58½"

From the remainder of the white solid, cut:
4 squares, 10¼" x 10¼"; cut into quarters diagonally to yield 16 triangles
16 squares, 5" x 5"

From *each* blue-and-white print, cut:
1 strip, 5" x 42"

From *each* blue solid, cut:
1 strip, 5" x 42";

From the blue print for binding, cut:
5 strips, 2¼" x 42"

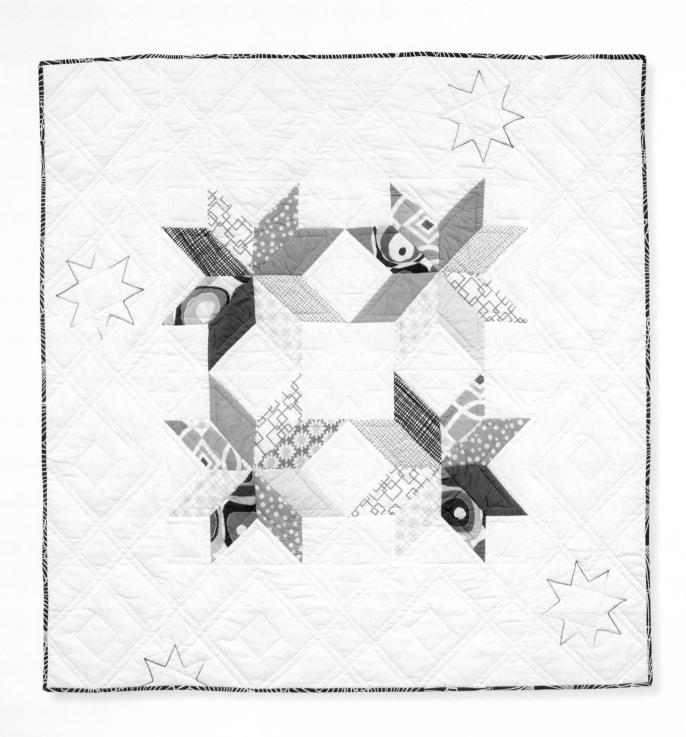

Designed and made by Victoria Findlay Wolfe

## CUTTING THE PARALLELOGRAMS

**1.** Fold one 5" strip in half with right sides together. Mark the lower edge every 5¼".

**2.** Lay a rotary-cutting ruler on the folded strip, aligning the ruler's edge with the first mark and the 45° line with the fabric edge. Cut the strip through both layers.

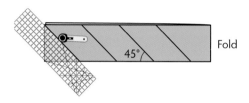

**3.** Slide the ruler along the fabric, making a parallel cut at each marking. You will be cutting pairs of mirror-image parallelograms. Cut 16 slanted in each direction, for a total of 32. If you wish, cut more parallelograms than required to give you more options when arranging the pieces.

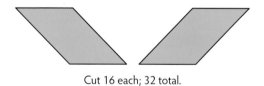

Cut 16 each; 32 total.

## MAKING THE BLOCKS

**1.** Arrange four eight-pointed stars on your design wall to get a good scrappy balance of colors, using at least one solid-color parallelogram in each star.

**2.** Sew a parallelogram to one side of a white triangle, stitching only between the seam-line intersections. Sew a second parallelogram to the adjacent side of the triangle, again sewing only between

the seam-line intersections. Sew the two parallelograms together, completing the Y-shaped seam.

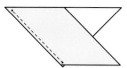

**3.** Add a white square to the first parallelogram in the unit. Make 16.

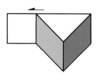

Make 16.

**4.** Sew two units together to make a half block; make eight. Assemble the half blocks to make four complete Star blocks.

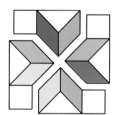 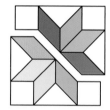

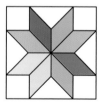

Star block.
Make 4.

## ASSEMBLING THE QUILT TOP

**1.** Sew the Star blocks together in two rows of two. Press the seam allowances to one side. Then sew the rows together. Press.

**2.** Sew the white 11½" x 36½" border strips to the top and bottom edges of the quilt center. Stitch a white 11½" x 58½" strip to each side. Press the seam allowances toward the border strips.

**3.** Trace the star pattern below onto template plastic and cut it out. Trace four stars onto the quilt top with a removable marking tool, using the quilt diagram as a guide. Position one star so that it appears to extend beyond the quilt's raw edges.

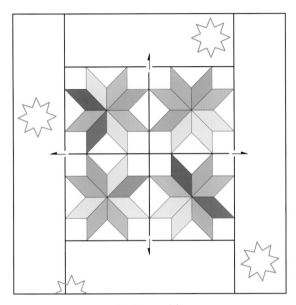

Quilt assembly

## FINISHING THE QUILT

For more information on finishing techniques, go to ShopMartingale.com/HowtoQuilt for free illustrated instructions.

**1.** Prepare the backing.

**2.** Layer the quilt top, batting, and backing, and baste the layers together. Quilt along the traced star outlines, and then finish stitching the quilt as desired. The sample quilt uses straight lines to echo the shapes and angles of the piecing.

**3.** Using a chain stitch and one strand of blue pearl cotton, stitch on top of the quilting to outline the stars in the borders.

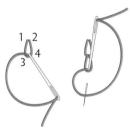

Chain stitch

**4.** Trim the backing and batting to match the quilt top.

**5.** Use the blue 2¼"-wide strips to bind the edges of the quilt. Add a label (if desired).

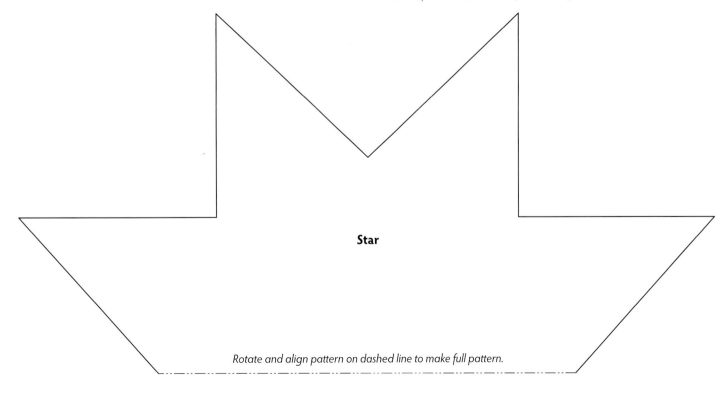

**Star**

*Rotate and align pattern on dashed line to make full pattern.*

# Square Dance

The colorful geometric design of this quilt is visually engaging for baby, with a style that's perfect for the modern parent. The size is large enough to grow from crib to toddler bed with your child.

~Lindsey

> **» Fabric Facts**
>
> Whether you use the colors listed or choose your own color palette, it's beneficial to make a list designating fabric 1, fabric 2, and so on, as a quick reference while piecing. Lindsey also found it very helpful to draw and color a quilt mock-up.

## MATERIALS

*Yardage is based on 42"-wide fabric.*

1 yard of charcoal solid for blocks and binding
¾ yard of teal solid for blocks
⅝ yard of orange solid for blocks
⅝ yard of light-blue solid for blocks
⅝ yard of green solid for blocks
⅝ yard of red solid for blocks
2¾ yards of fabric for backing
46" x 62" piece of batting

## CUTTING

*A ¼" seam allowance is included in all measurements.*

From the teal solid, cut:
5 squares, 9¼" x 9¼"
7 rectangles, 3" x 8½"
1 rectangle, 3½" x 6"
1 rectangle, 3" x 3½"
3 rectangles, 3" x 6"
1 square, 6" x 6"

From the orange solid, cut:
2 squares, 9¼" x 9¼"
3 squares, 6½" x 6½"
5 rectangles, 3" x 8½"
1 rectangle, 3½" x 6"
1 rectangle, 3" x 3½"
2 rectangles, 3" x 6"
3 squares, 6" x 6"

From the light-blue solid, cut:
2 squares, 9¼" x 9¼"
3 squares, 6½" x 6½"
4 rectangles, 3" x 8½"
1 rectangle, 3½" x 6"
2 rectangles, 3" x 6"
3 squares, 6" x 6"

*Continued on page 68*

Designed and made by Lindsey Rhodes

From the charcoal solid, cut:
3 squares, 9¼" x 9¼"
2 squares, 6½" x 6½"
6 rectangles, 3" x 8½"
3 rectangles, 3" x 6"
2 squares, 6" x 6"
6 strips, 2¼" x 42"

From the green solid, cut:
2 squares, 9¼" x 9¼"
3 squares, 6½" x 6½"
5 rectangles, 3" x 8½"
1 rectangle, 3" x 3½"
2 rectangles, 3" x 6"
3 squares, 6" x 6"

From the red solid, cut:
2 squares, 9¼" x 9¼"
3 squares, 6½" x 6½"
5 rectangles, 3" x 8½"
1 rectangle, 3½" x 6"
1 rectangle, 3" x 3½"
2 rectangles, 3" x 6"
2 squares, 6" x 6"

## MAKING THE HALF-SQUARE-TRIANGLE UNITS

1. Place a teal 9¼" square on an orange 9¼" square, right sides together and raw edges aligned. Sew around all four sides as shown. Cut along both diagonals, creating four half-square-triangle units.

 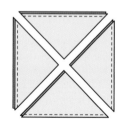

Stitch.                     Cut apart.

Press.

2. Repeat step 1, pairing a teal square with a light-blue square; teal with charcoal; teal with green; teal with red; orange with charcoal; light-blue with charcoal; and green with red. Make four half-square-triangle units of each combination, for a total of 32. You will use only 27 units in the quilt; save the extras for another project.

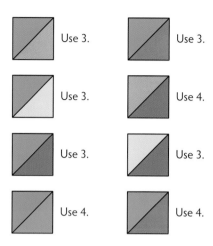

Use 3.          Use 3.
Use 3.          Use 4.
Use 3.          Use 3.
Use 4.          Use 4.

> ## » In the Stretch
> Half-square triangles constructed in steps 1 and 2 have bias edges, so be careful not to stretch the pieces as you stitch and press.

3. Pair an orange 6½" square with a light-blue 6½" square, right sides together and raw edges aligned. Draw a line from corner to corner on the wrong side of the light-blue square. Stitch ¼" from the line on both sides. Cut along the diagonal line to create two half-square-triangle units.

Mark.          Stitch.          Cut apart.

Press.

**4.** Repeat step 3, pairing an orange square with a green square; orange with red; light blue with green; light blue with red; charcoal with green; and charcoal with red. Make two half-square-triangle units of each combination, for a total of 14. You will have one extra orange/light-blue unit.

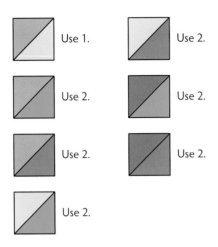

Use 1. Use 2. Use 2. Use 2. Use 2. Use 2. Use 2.

**5.** Square up and trim each half-square-triangle unit to 5¾" x 5¾".

## MAKING THE SQUARE DANCE BLOCKS

**1.** Sew a light-blue 3" x 6" rectangle to an orange 6" square. Sew light-blue 3" x 8½" rectangles to opposite sides of the assembled unit. Make 14 full Square Dance blocks, referring to the quilt diagram on page 70 for color combinations.

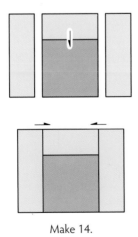

Make 14.

**2.** Sew a green 3" x 3½" rectangle to a teal 3½" x 6" rectangle. Sew a green 3" x 8½" rectangle to the right edge of the unit. Make another half block, this time sewing red rectangles to two edges of an orange rectangle.

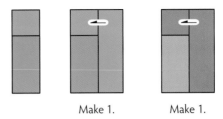

Make 1. Make 1.

**3.** Repeat step 2 to make two more half blocks in the color combinations shown, adding the 3" x 8½" rectangles to the left edge of the assembled units.

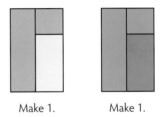

Make 1. Make 1.

## ASSEMBLING THE QUILT TOP

Refer to the quilt diagram for guidance with color placement.

**1.** Arrange the half-square-triangle units in five rows of eight units each. Carefully match the points and sew the units together into rows.

> **» Walk This Way**
>
> Because most of the half-square-triangle units have bias edges, a walking foot is helpful when joining the units.

**2.** Referring to the quilt diagram, arrange the full and half Square Dance blocks in four rows of four blocks each (counting the half blocks at the ends of two of the rows as one block). Turn alternating blocks upside down to create the "dance," as shown in the quilt assembly diagram. Sew the blocks together into rows.

**3.** Sew the rows together, alternating half-square-triangle rows with Square Dance rows. Press all the seam allowances downward.

## FINISHING THE QUILT

For more information on finishing techniques, go to ShopMartingale.com/HowtoQuilt for free illustrated instructions.

**1.** Prepare the backing.

**2.** Layer the quilt top, batting, and backing, and baste the layers together. Quilt as desired.

**3.** Trim the backing and batting to match the quilt top.

**4.** Use the charcoal 2¼"-wide strips to bind the edges of the quilt. Add a label (if desired).

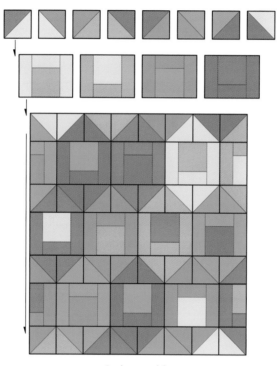

Quilt assembly

# Jazzed-Up Tumbling Blocks

**FINISHED QUILT: 40½" x 40½"   FINISHED BLOCK: 10" x 10"**

I love reinterpreting traditional quilt designs, and there's something inherently modern about tumbling blocks—striking, geometric, and optically playful. I've incorporated stripes and slanting borders for a multidimensional visual effect. The simplified method for creating the individual blocks is borrowed from Marci Baker. The border piecing is unconventional and leaves scraps, but it makes for easier measuring—and resourceful quilters always work wonders with their leftover bits!

~ Pippa

## »Fabric Facts

This rich and complex design works best in solid fabrics and bold hues. Sample fabrics are Robert Kaufman Kona Cotton Solids. When choosing fabrics for your quilt, aim for plenty of contrast within a range of three values per color.

## MATERIALS

*Yardage is based on 42"-wide fabric unless otherwise noted.*

½ yard *each* of 10 different solid colors for blocks: 2 shades (light and dark) *each* of orange, green, blue, purple, and red*

¼ yard *each* of 5 different medium-value solid colors for blocks: orange, green, blue, purple, and red*

⅜ yard of dark-gray solid for binding

1⅜ yards of 60"-wide flannel for backing**

46" x 46" piece of batting

*You can interpret the shades somewhat loosely; for example, the dark red in the sample quilt is actually a brown.*

**Pippa likes to use 60"-wide flannel to avoid a seam in the backing fabric for smaller quilts, but you could also piece the backing from 2⅝ yards of 42"-wide fabric.*

## CUTTING

*A ¼" seam allowance is included in all measurements unless otherwise specified.*

### From the light-orange solid, cut:

10 strips, 1" x 42"; crosscut 2 strips into 8 rectangles, 1" x 8". Reserve the remaining strips for background piecing.

2 rectangles, 3" x 8"

1 square, 4" x 4"

1 rectangle, 5½" x 7"

### From the medium-orange solid, cut:

2 strips, 1" x 42"; crosscut into 8 rectangles, 1" x 8"

2 rectangles, 3" x 8"

1 rectangle, 4" x 7"

1 rectangle, 4" x 10"

### From the dark-orange solid, cut:

11 strips, 1" x 42"; crosscut 2 strips into 8 rectangles, 1" x 8". Reserve the remaining strips for background piecing.

2 rectangles, 3" x 8"

1 rectangle, 3½" x 8"

1 rectangle, 3½" x 12"

*Continued on page 73*

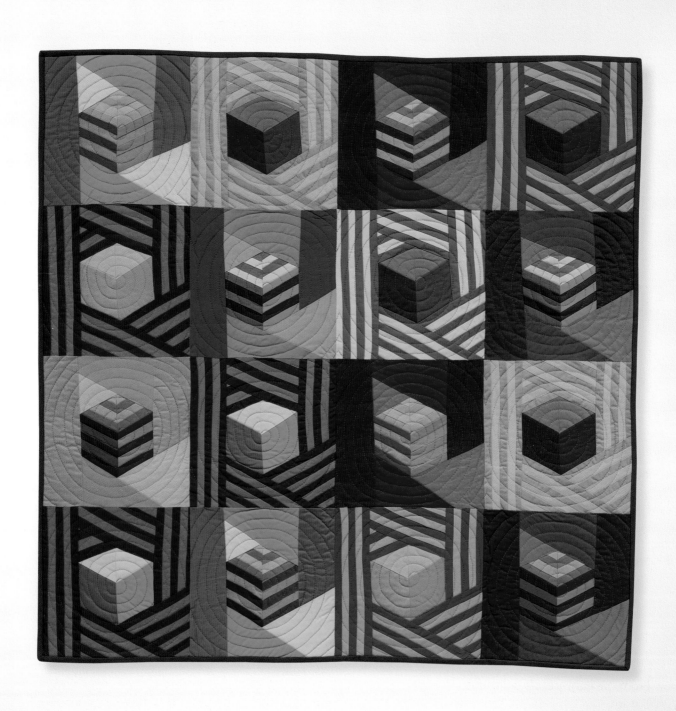

Designed and made by Pippa Eccles Armbrester

Jazzed-Up Tumbling Blocks

From the light-green solid, cut:

6 strips, 1" x 42"; crosscut 2 strips into 6 rectangles, 1" x 8". Reserve the remaining strips for background piecing.
2 rectangles, 3" x 8"
2 squares, 4" x 4"
2 rectangles, 5½" x 7"

From the medium-green solid, cut:

2 strips, 1" x 42"; crosscut into 6 rectangles, 1" x 8"
2 rectangles, 3" x 8"
2 rectangles, 4" x 7"
2 rectangles, 4" x 10"

From the dark-green solid, cut:

7 strips, 1" x 42"; crosscut 2 strips into 6 rectangles, 1" x 8". Reserve the remaining strips for background piecing.
2 rectangles, 3" x 8"
2 rectangles, 3½" x 8"
2 rectangles, 3½" x 12"

From the light-blue solid, cut:

11 strips, 1" x 42"; crosscut 3 strips into 10 rectangles, 1" x 8". Reserve the remaining strips for background piecing.
1 square, 4" x 4"
1 rectangle, 5½" x 7"

From the medium-blue solid, cut:

3 strips, 1" x 42"; crosscut into 10 rectangles, 1" x 8"
1 rectangle, 4" x 7"
1 rectangle, 4" x 10"

From the dark-blue solid, cut:

12 strips, 1" x 42"; crosscut 3 strips into 10 rectangles, 1" x 8". Reserve the remaining strips for background piecing.
1 rectangle, 3½" x 8"
1 rectangle, 3½" x 12"

From the light-purple solid, cut:

6 strips, 1" x 42"; crosscut 2 strips into 6 rectangles, 1" x 8". Reserve the remaining strips for background piecing.
2 rectangles, 3" x 8"
2 squares, 4" x 4"
2 rectangles, 5½" x 7"

From the medium-purple solid, cut:

2 strips, 1" x 42"; crosscut into 6 rectangles, 1" x 8"
2 rectangles, 3" x 8"
2 rectangles, 4" x 7"
2 rectangles, 4" x 10"

From the dark-purple solid, cut:

7 strips, 1" x 42"; crosscut 2 strips into 6 rectangles, 1" x 8". Reserve the remaining strips for background piecing.
2 rectangles, 3" x 8"
2 rectangles, 3½" x 8"
2 rectangles, 3½" x 12"

From the light-red solid, cut:

11 strips, 1" x 42"; crosscut 3 strips into 10 rectangles, 1" x 8". Reserve the remaining strips for background piecing.
2 rectangles, 3" x 8"
2 squares, 4" x 4"
2 rectangles, 5½" x 7"

From the medium-red solid, cut:

3 strips, 1" x 42"; crosscut into 10 rectangles, 1" x 8"
2 rectangles, 3" x 8"
2 rectangles, 4" x 7"
2 rectangles, 4" x 10"

From the dark-red solid, cut:

12 strips, 1" x 42"; crosscut 3 strips into 10 rectangles, 1" x 8". Reserve the remaining strips for background piecing.
2 rectangles, 3" x 8"
2 rectangles, 3½" x 8"
2 rectangles, 3½" x 12"

From the dark-gray solid, cut:

5 strips, 2¼" x 42"

## MAKING THE STRIPED TUMBLING BLOCKS

**1.** Sew a dark-orange 1" x 8" rectangle to a dark-blue 1" x 8" rectangle; press the seam allowances away from the dark-blue rectangle. Make four. Sew the units together in two groups of two. Add a dark-blue 1" x 8" rectangle to the orange side of each group, and press the seam allowances in one direction.

**2.** Sew a light-orange 1" x 8" rectangle to a light-blue 1" x 8" rectangle; press the seam allowances away from the light-blue rectangle. Make two. Sew the two units together and add a light-blue 1" x 8" rectangle to the orange edge. Sew the dark units from step 1 to the long sides of the light unit, and press all the seam allowances in one direction.

**3.** Repeat steps 1 and 2, substituting medium-orange and medium-blue 1" x 8" rectangles for the darks. Press the seam allowances in one direction.

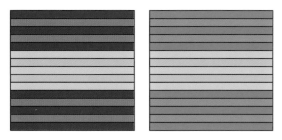

Make 1 of each.

**4.** Trim the right end of the dark strip set at a 60° angle as shown. Use the angled mark on your ruler as a guide, or use a triangular rotary ruler. Trim the right end of the light strip set at a 60° angle in the opposite direction, as shown.

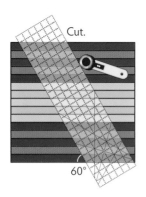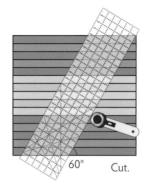

**5.** Cut a 3" strip from the angled end of each strip set, and draw a diagonal line as shown, from corner to corner across the lighter center area. Cut along the line to divide each strip in half.

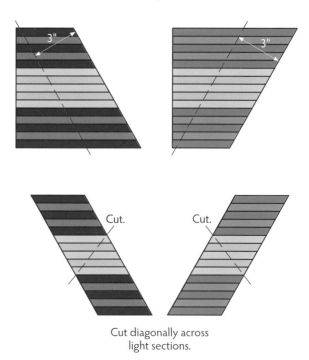

Cut diagonally across light sections.

**6.** Pair one dark/light unit and one medium/light unit from step 5, and stitch them together. Press the seam allowances open. Make two.

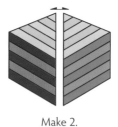

Make 2.

**7.** Repeat steps 1–7 to create two tumbling blocks each with green and red, purple and orange, and red and blue strips. Refer closely to the quilt photo on page 72 for color placement. You will have a total of eight striped tumbling blocks.

## MAKING THE QUILT BLOCKS

**1.** Sew a light-green 4" square to the upper-left edge of a blue-and-orange tumbling block. Press the seam allowances toward the square. Align a rotary-cutting ruler with the upper-right edge of the tumbling block and trim the green square to match the side of the tumbling block, as shown.

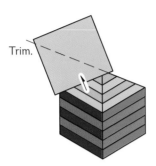

Trim.

**2.** Sew a medium-green 4" x 7" rectangle to the side just trimmed, and press the rectangle away from the tumbling block. Trim the new rectangle to match the tumbling block as before.

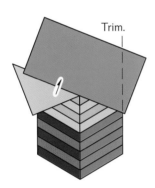

Trim.

### » Losing a Strip

When adding the surrounding border fabrics, you'll find that the strip at the top of the tumbling block disappears into the seam allowances, so the light area of the block consists of just four alternating strips rather than the original five.

**3.** Working in a clockwise direction, continue sewing and trimming rectangles, adding a dark-green 3½" x 8" rectangle, a light-green 5½" x 7" rectangle, a medium-green 4" x 10" rectangle, and a dark-green 3½" x 12" rectangle. Before adding the last rectangle, trim the entire left side of the unit, creating a straight edge for seaming, and center the last background rectangle on the striped tumbling block.

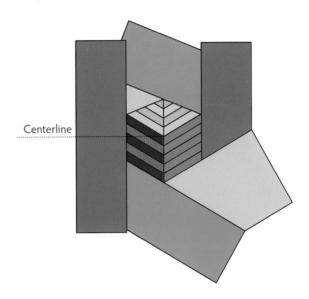

Centerline

**4.** Using a large square rotary-cutting ruler, trim the block to 10½" x 10½", aligning the central point of the tumbling block (where the light, medium, and dark segments meet) with the 5¼" x 5¼" point on the ruler.

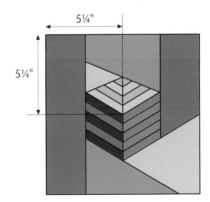

5¼"

5¼"

Trim to 10½" x 10½".

**5.** Repeat steps 1–4 to create seven more quilt blocks from the striped tumbling blocks. Refer to the diagram on page 78 and the quilt photo for color placement. Note that even though there are two tumbling blocks of each color combination, they are surrounded by different colors. No two blocks are alike.

## MAKING THE SOLID TUMBLING BLOCKS

**1.** Sew a dark-purple 3" x 8" rectangle to each long edge of a light-purple 3" x 8" rectangle. Press the seam allowances toward the dark-purple rectangles. Sew a medium-purple 3" x 8" rectangle to each long edge of the remaining light-purple rectangle. Press the seam allowances toward the light-purple rectangle.

**2.** Trim the right edge of the dark/light/dark unit at a 60° angle as shown. Trim the right edge of the medium/light/medium unit at a 60° angle in the opposite direction, as shown.

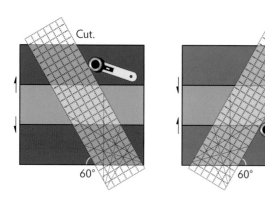

**3.** Cut a 3" strip from the angled edge of each unit, and then cut across the diagonal of the light center strip as shown, from corner to corner, to divide each strip in half.

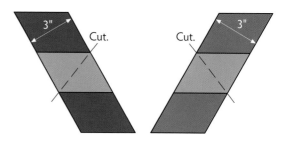

Cut diagonally across center sections.

**4.** Align dark/light and medium/light units as shown and stitch together to make a tumbling block. Press the seam allowances open. Make two.

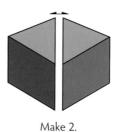

Make 2.

**5.** Repeat steps 1–4 to create two tumbling blocks each in orange, red, and green, for a total of eight solid tumbling blocks.

## MAKING THE ALTERNATE BLOCKS

**1.** Cut a 4" segment from the end of a dark-orange 1" x 42" strip, and sew the segment to the upper-left edge of a purple tumbling block. Press the seam allowances away from the tumbling block. Use scissors to cut the end of the strip just past the edge of the tumbling block; leave the strip a bit longer than necessary to give yourself some wiggle room.

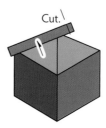

Cut.

The technique used for adding the stripes around the solid tumbling blocks is quite freewheeling. If you loathe the idea of lots of leftover fabric, trim the strips more precisely as you work. Pippa finds it helpful to have one of the completed striped blocks nearby to use as a reference for determining how long the strips need to be.

It's easiest to begin with 42"-long strips and trim them so they roughly align with the tumbling-block edges as you go, rather than measuring and cutting beforehand. Always begin by sewing a dark, and then a light, and alternate between the two.

**2.** Cut a light-orange strip about 3" long and sew it to the dark-orange strip; press the seam allowances away from the dark orange. Roughly trim this strip to align with the tumbling block. Add another dark-orange strip and another light-orange strip, roughly trimming as you go. Align a ruler with the upper-right edge of the tumbling block and trim the strips in line with the tumbling block.

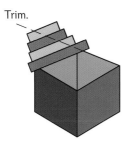

**3.** Add orange strips to the upper-right edge of the tumbling block in the same way. Begin with a dark strip and alternate dark and light, attaching a total of six strips. Trim the strips to align with the tumbling block.

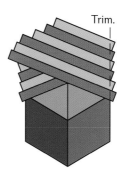

**4.** Working clockwise, sew five orange strips to the next side of the tumbling block, beginning with a dark strip and alternating dark and light. Trim precisely along the edge of the tumbling block when complete. Sew nine strips to the next side of the tumbling block, and then seven strips, and then five strips to the final edge. Always begin with a dark strip. Trim the entire left side of the block before adding the final set of strips.

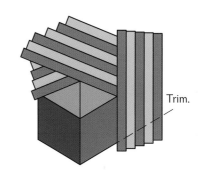

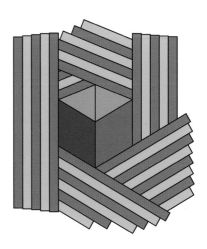

**5.** Trim the block to 10½" x 10½", aligning the central point of the tumbling block with the 5¼" x 5¼" point on the ruler.

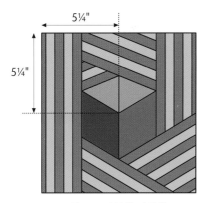

Trim to 10½" x 10½".

**6.** Repeat steps 1–5 to create seven more blocks, referring to the photo and diagram for color combinations.

## ASSEMBLING THE QUILT TOP

**1.** Arrange the blocks in four rows of four blocks each, alternating solid and striped tumbling blocks. Arrange the colors as shown in the quilt assembly diagram, right, or as desired.

**2.** Sew the blocks together in rows, pressing the seam allowances open or in alternating directions from row to row. Sew the rows together, pressing the seam allowances open or all in one direction.

Quilt assembly

## FINISHING THE QUILT

For more information on finishing techniques, go to ShopMartingale.com/HowtoQuilt for free illustrated instructions.

**1.** Prepare the backing.

**2.** Layer the quilt top, batting, and backing, and baste the layers together. Quilt as desired. The sample quilt features a curlicue in each block, with a spiraling diamond pattern filling the empty spaces at the block intersections.

**3.** Trim the backing and batting to match the quilt top.

**4.** Use the dark-gray 2¼"-wide strips to bind the edges of the quilt. Add a label (if desired).

# About the Contributors

## » Pippa Eccles Armbrester

Pippa is a quiltmaker and designer with a fondness for bold geometric designs and bright, colorful solid fabrics, focusing on patterns that balance the tradition of quilting and patchwork with a fun, whimsical, and contemporary approach. She believes in a fuss-free and joyful attitude regarding the quiltmaking process, one that emphasizes heartfelt quilts meant to be used rather than so-called perfect technique. She lives and works in Boston with her husband, Kyle; her floppy-eared bunnies, Shuffle and Stitch; and her tiny teacup poodle, Martin. Pippa enjoys cooking and baking (bread especially), attends frequent hot-yoga classes, and loves long (but slow) runs by the Charles River. Knitting and crochet are her portable needlework of choice. She blogs at PippaPatchwork.com and sells her quilts online at www.etsy.com/shop/PippaPatchwork.

## » Audrie Bidwell

Born in Singapore and raised in Australia, Audrie found quilting after she moved to the United States. Quilting was the perfect outlet for her creativity, and has led her to a community she is proud to be part of. She does not come from a crafty family but taught herself to sew and knit. (She still can't draw to save her life.) Audrie loves working with bright colors and drawing inspiration from traditional designs. She lives in Connecticut with her husband and two Ragdoll kitties. You can find her online at BlueIsBleu.blogspot.com, where she chronicles her life and loves.

## » Carrie Bloomston

Carrie is an artist, designer, abstract painter, and sewist. After studying painting at the Rhode Island School of Design, she owned a mural-painting business for 16 years. Now, when not hanging out with her inspiring kids and thoughtful husband, she is wearing a bunch of hats for her new sewing-pattern company, SUCH Designs. "Everything I do is for my kids, because of my kids, or with my kids. My family is my reason," Carries says. "My goal is to help people to sew simple, artful stuff. Think of me as your inner-artist enabler. I want to help you celebrate your inner artist!" See more of Carrie's designs at Such-Designs.com.

## » Dana Bolyard

Dana has blogged since 2007, finding it the perfect platform for cultivating and capturing a creative life. She likes that blogging allows her to put a date stamp on what matters to her at any given moment—whether it relates to motherhood, quilting, soap making, photography, or simply the average daily routine right here, right now. Documenting the quilts she makes is an added bonus! Find out more of what Dana is designing, sewing, quilting, and possibly even pondering, at OldRedBarnCo.blogspot.com.

## » Melissa Corry

Melissa has always loved quilting as a hobby. Then she discovered the amazing virtual quilting community and her quilting grew from a hobby to a business, Happy Quilting. It began in 2010 as a blog (HappyQuiltingMelissa.blogspot.com). After a little while, Melissa started doing tutorials, which then expanded into creating and selling her own patterns, which in turn led to being a contributor to this book. Melissa says Happy Quilting is growing in leaps and bounds and she's looking forward to seeing where it takes her next.

## » Jen Eskridge

Jen is a designer who has been quilting and sewing for over half her life. She is a military spouse to a fabulous guy currently on active duty in the Air National Guard. While her husband was on active duty in the United States Air Force, Jen had the opportunity to live in five different cities—including Daegu, South Korea—in just 10 years. Jen graduated from Louisiana State University in 1998 with a degree in apparel design and is the owner/designer of the pattern company ReannaLily Designs. The company invented and launched the Seamingly Accurate Seam Guide in 2008. Many published patterns and magazine features have followed, as well as a quilting book. Along with books and patterns, Jen maintains her website and blog at ReannaLilyDesigns.com.

## » Jake Finch

Jake has been addicted to fabric since she could say, "Mine!" The author of four books and a contributor to numerous others, Jake has been a designer and teacher for many years. But it's her other hat that's really fun. With the support of a small army of fellow fabric addicts, Jake is the creator and publisher of *Generation Q,* an online and print magazine that celebrates creative stitching, especially quilts, with fun and sass. Jake lives in Southern California with her hubby, 11-year-old daughter, five cats, and six fish. She can be found at MamaMakesQuilts.com or at GenerationQMagazine.com.

## » Sarah Flynn

Sarah lives in Cork, Ireland, with her husband and children. By day, she works in the field of human resources, but her free time is spent on family, quilting, and blogging. Despite a strong family tradition of crafting, she only started sewing in 2008, and quilting in 2010. She immediately fell in love with modern quilting and fabrics and soon began experimenting with her own designs. She is now an unrepentant quilting and fabric addict! She loves clean, simple design and playing with color. Sarah blogs at FairyFaceDesigns.blogspot.com.

## » Carolyn Friedlander

Carolyn designs quilts and fabric from her hometown of Lake Wales, Florida, an environment she enjoys for its warm weather, few distractions, and thriving community of quilters and crafters. She loves to both learn from and teach others. In her work, she draws inspiration from features of the Florida landscape—its longleaf pines, palmettos, water, scrub land, sand—as well as the architecture, history, and cultural identity of St. Louis, Missouri, where she studied and practiced architecture for several years.

## » Shea Henderson

Shea is owner of the pattern company Empty Bobbin Sewing Studio, based in Kansas City, Missouri. She is a former middle-school math teacher turned sewing-pattern designer—two careers that are, surprisingly, not so different from each other! Her sewing patterns are carried in stores across the country and around the world. When not designing, Shea can be found raising two precocious preschoolers with her husband, or sewing up a storm with her fellow members of the Kansas City Modern Quilt Guild, of which she is president and cofounder. Find more of Shea's work at EmptyBobbinSewing.com.

## » Lindsey Rhodes

Lindsey was born in Dallas, Texas, and grew up always dabbling in something crafty. She taught herself to sew at the age of 16 after inheriting an old Singer sewing machine. Her grandmother had written Lindsey's name on the underside of the machine, and that small gesture sparked an enduring love of sewing, quilting, and pattern design. Lindsey now resides in Atlanta, Georgia, with her husband and two small children. Her family members are her biggest fans and are forever patient about finding stray threads on just about everything! You can read about Lindsey's quilting and design at LRstitched.com.

## » Amy Smart

Growing up, Amy learned to sew from her mom, but it wasn't until she had her first baby 14 years ago that she really started quilting with a vengeance. In 2008, when Amy discovered blogs written by other sewists, she felt like she'd found a bunch of new best friends. She started writing her own blog later that year (visit her at DiaryofaQuilter.com) and has thoroughly enjoyed connecting with the online quilting community. Behind the scenes, Amy's a wife to a patient husband, as well as mom to four active kids. The family lives in Utah where they love hiking, visiting national parks, and playing with LEGO.

## » Victoria Findlay Wolfe

After discovering quilt blogs in 2008, Victoria wanted to be part of a community of quilters who were making quilts that excited her. In order to share her quilting obsession with others, she started a blog BumbleBeansInc.blogspot.com. She also maintains 15MinutesPlay.com, a place where she describes her process for designing unique quilts, while hopefully inspiring and challenging other quilters on their own quilting adventures! Victoria's business is focused on making custom quilts and giving back to the community. As someone who is so grateful to do what she loves, she feels it's important to share that joy with others through quilts.